# COUNTRY STUDIES

# INDIA

## Steve Brace

### Series Editor: John Hopkin

Heinemann

Heinemann Library
Halley Court, Jordan Hill, Oxford OX2 8EJ
a division of Reed Educational & Professional Publishing Ltd
Heinemann is a registered trademark of Reed Educational & Professional Publishing Ltd.

OXFORD FLORENCE PRAGUE MADRID ATHENS
MELBOURNE AUCKLAND KUALA LUMPUR SINGAPORE TOKYO
IBADAN NAIROBI KAMPALA JOHANNESBURG GABORONE
PORTSMOUTH NH (USA) CHICAGO MEXICO CITY SAO PAOLO

First published 1998

00 99 98
10 9 8 7 6 5 4 3 2 1

British Library Cataloguing in Publication Data
Brace, Steve
    India. - (Country Studies)
    1.India - Social conditions - (1947) - Juvenile literature
    2.India - History - (1947) - Juvenile literature
    3.India - Description and travel - Juvenile literature
    I.Title II.ActionAid
    954'.052

Hardback ISBN 0 431 01406 X
Paperback ISBN 0 431 01407 8

Typeset and illustrated by Hardlines, Charlbury, Oxford OX7 3PS
Printed and bound in Spain by Mateu Cromo

### Acknowledgements

The publisher would like to thank the following for permission to reproduce copyright material.

Maps and extracts
**p.5** *India Year Book*, 1995; **p.6 A** Salil Shetty, ACTIONAID-India; **p.6** *Lonely Planet Guide to India*; **p.6** *Daily Mail, 7 September* 1995; **p.7** extract adapted from *Understanding Global Issues* 97/1; **p.10** *Lonely Planet Guide to India*; **p.14** Dr Lohiya from Manavlok, an Indian development charity; **p.16** *India Year Book*; **p.17** *The Economist*, 1997; **p.23** *The Independent*, 19 March 1995; **p.24** *Lonely Planet Guide to India*; **p.26 B** data from *The Economist*; **p.28** *Financial Times*; **p.29** *The Economist*, 1997; **p.30** Kanwar Sain, chief engineer of the Indira Gandhi Canal; **p.36 A and B** 1994 World Bank Development Report; **p.36** extracts adapted from *The Financial Times*, 8 November 1994 and *Understanding Global Issues*; **p.41** *International Herald Tribune*; **p.43 C** *Global Eye*, Issue 4 Autumn 1997; **p.43** Philip D'Souza of *The New Internationalist*; **p.45** Clive Anderson, BBC film, *Our Man in Goa*; **p.45 D** cartoon from Tourism Concern; **p.45** Tourism Concern; **p.46** *The Economist*; **p.47** *The New Internationalist*; **p.49** Adapted from *The New Internationalist* and *Understanding Global Issues*; **p.51** United Nations Industrial Development Organization; **p.53** Binu S Thomas, ACTIONAID-India; **p.55** *The Daily Telegraph*, 10 September 1997; **p.57 C** *Financial Times*, 6 September 1995; **p.57** The Indian Centre for Science and Environment; **p.57** *The Economist*, 1997; **p.58** *The Economist*.

Photos
**p.4 A** Robert Harding Picture Library; **p.4 B** Nigel Hicks; **p.5 C** Science Photo Library; **p.6 A** ACTIONAID; **p.6 B** Hutchison Library; **p.7 C** Hutchison Library; **p.8 A** British Library; **p.9 B** British Library; **p.9 C** Victoria and Albert Museum; **p.10 A** Panos Pictures; **p.10 B** ACTIONAID; **p.12 A** Hutchison Library; **p.13 B** Kumar-Unep/Still Pictures; **p.14 A** ACTIONAID; **p.16 A** Panos Pictures; **p.20 A** Images of India Picture Library; **p.22 A** Dinodia Picture Library; **p.22 B** Panos Pictures; **p.24 B** ACTIONAID; **p.26 A** ZUL; **p.27 C** Robert Harding Picture Library; **p.28 A** Panos Pictures; **p.28 B** Dinodia Picture Library; **p.29 D** Images of India Picture Library; **p.30 A** ImageBank; **p.31 B** Still Pictures; **p.32 A** Still Pictures; **p.33 B** ACTIONAID; **p.34 A** Still Pictures; **p.34 B** ACTIONAID; **p.37 C** ACTIONAID; **p.37 D** Images of India Picture Library; **p.38 A** Images of India Picture Library; **p.39 B** Hulton-Deutsch Collection; **p.40 B** AP/Agit Kumar; **p.41 F** Associated Press Ltd; **p.42 A** Dinodia Picture Library; **p.42 B** Dinodia Picture Library; **p.44 A** Images of India Picture Library; **p.48 A** Images of India Picture Library; **p.48 B** ACTIONAID; **p.50 B** Images of India Picture Library; **p.50 C** Ann and Bury Peerless; **p.52 A** Still Pictures; **p.54 A** Still Pictures; **p.56 A** Hulton Getty Picture Library; **p.57 B** Hutchison Library; **p.58 A** Robert Harding Picture Library; **p.59 B** Images of India Picture Library.

# Contents

## India's landscapes

▶ How is India's land laid out?

▶ What are India's main landscapes?

### India's physical geography

India's landscape can be divided into a number of different areas. Along India's northern border are the Himalayas. The highest point in India is Kanchenjunga at 8598 metres. Everest's peak (8848m) is in Nepal. To the south of these mountains are the wide fertile plains of the Ganges valley. In the west is the Thar desert. Stretching across central, and down into southern India, is the Deccan Plateau. This is an area of raised flat land about 1000 metres high, which is bordered by the highlands of the Eastern and Western Ghats.

Within these areas there are many contrasting environmental regions. The Thar desert has less than 300mm rainfall a year, but Cherrapunji in the state of Meghalaya is the wettest place in the world, receiving 11 437mm (over 11 metres!) a year.

**B** The wide river valleys and flat low-lying lands which are found across the Bay of Bengal.

800km south of the heights of the Himalayas, the Ganges drains into the Bay of Bengal creating a huge flat delta, where thousands of hectares are only a few centimetres above sea level.

**A** Bhagirathi Parbat showing the high peaks and glaciers in the Indian Himalayas.

**C  A satellite image showing the Indian sub-continent**

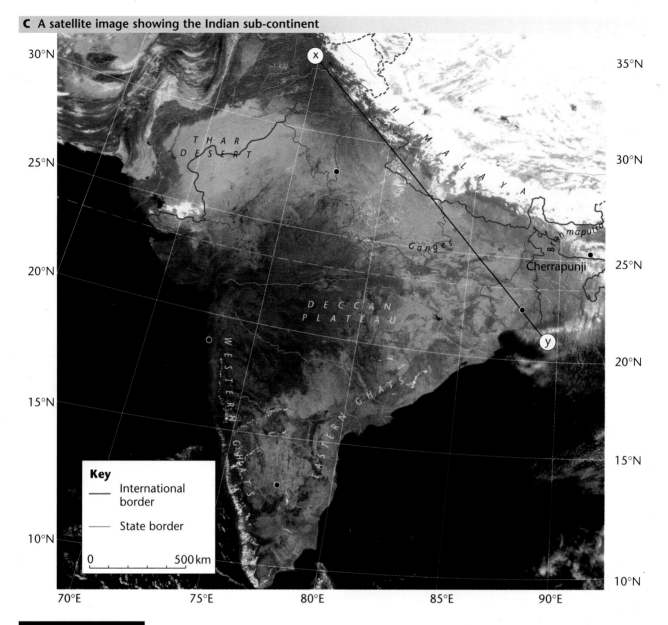

**Key**
— International border
— State border

0 ———— 500 km

## FACTFILE

**Mountains, deserts, plains, and deltas**

'India occupies a strategic position in Asia, looking across the seas to Arabia and Africa on the west and to Burma, Malaysia and the Indonesian archipelago on the east. Geographically, the Himalayan ranges kept India apart from the rest of Asia.  The fertility of the Indo-Gangetic belt, however, has proved to be such an irresistible magnet that hordes of people have pressed into India through the mountain passes from ancient times. India has a land frontier of 15 200km and a coastline of 7 516km. All the major land forms – hills, mountains, plateaus and plains are well represented in India.'

*India Year Book*, 1995

The borders of four contrasting regions have been included in the satellite image above. Rajasthan lies in the north-west of India and borders Pakistan. It is largely desert. The Thar desert stretches across hundreds of kilometers. West Bengal lies in the Ganges delta. Its lands are fertile and it is one of the most populated regions. Jammu and Kashmir is a state or region in the Himalayan mountain range. It borders China. Farming is almost impossible here. Uttar Pradesh lies in the centre of northern India in fertile lowlands. The Ganges river flows through it. The land is flat and ideal for farming.

# India's people

## ▶ What is India's human geography like?

### India's diverse people

'India is the world's ninth most industrialized country, with the scientific power to launch its own satellites. Its 200 million middle classes would be the envy of any developing country. India has the potential to become an economic tiger, but it is also one of the world's poorest nations.'

Salil Shetty, ACTIONAID-India

'India captures the imagination. From Rajasthan's deserts to the Himalayas, from holy cows to Bengal tigers – India's extraordinary diversity fascinates travellers.'

Lonely Planet Guide to India

**A** Sampangi, one of Bangalore's many rag pickers, who collect waste paper and plastic to be sold for recycling.

People in Europe sometimes describe India as a 'developing' country, focusing on images of poverty. People also think of India as the source of products like tea, spices or cotton, or as being famous for the exotic Taj Mahal. But India has a great wealth of natural and human resources. In fact there is as much diversity in this one country as you would find across the whole of Europe.

**B** A Calcutta family, who are part of India's 200 million strong middle classes, enjoying a meal together.

**Languages:** there are 1652 Indian 'mother tongue languages', with 33 being spoken by more than one million people. Hindi is the official language and English is widely spoken.

**Wealth:** India's **Gross National Product Capita** is $290 per person per year, compared to $17 970 in Britain. GNP measures the average amount of wealth created by each person. Not everyone has the same amount of money, and India's population includes the super-rich and people who survive on 50p a day.

**Religions:** many religions are found here including Hinduism, Islam, Buddhism and Sikhism. There are also communities of Christians, Jains and Adivasis. Most Indians are Hindus and belong to **castes**. There are four main groups of castes arranged in a hierarchy. Below these are the Scheduled Castes, who often face discrimination. The government outlawed discrimination and provided them with job quotas and political seats.

**Guests Gather for £4m Wedding Feast**
'By comparison, even royal weddings look paltry – the guest list runs to 300 000. This £4 million extravagance is being put on by Jayalalitha Jauaram, former film star and chief minister of Tamil Nadu.'

Daily Mail 7 September 1995

**C** People gathering for the festival of Holi in Ahore, Rajasthan.

**Gender:** Indira Gandhi, who was twice India's Prime Minister (1966–77 and 1980–84), shows how women can rise to the highest levels of society. However, despite her achievements, there remains a gap between the quality of life of men and women. For example, while 64 per cent of men can read and write, only 36 per cent of women can.

For geographers India's **diversity** makes it an important country to study. Your investigations will help you find out how and why India is changing. Then you can write your own description of India.

| Religion | % of population |
| --- | --- |
| Hindu | 83 |
| Muslim | 11 |
| Christian | 2.5 |
| Sikh | 2.5 |
| Buddhist | 1 |

**D** India's main regions

## FACTFILE

### Hinduism and the system

Hinduism is partly a religion and partly a social system. The three most important gods are Brahma, Vishnu and Shiva, although thousands of other gods are also worshiped. Hindus have two basic beliefs: *reincarnation* (believers come back in a different life) and *dharma*, a belief in natural laws and religious and personal duty.

India has 800 million Hindus: 23 per cent belong to the upper castes, 57 per cent are in the backward castes, and 20 per cent are untouchables. At the top were the Brahmins (priests), the Kshatriyas (landowners) and Vaishyas (merchants). The caste system laid down strict rules about how society was organized and how different groups should behave, rather like the class system in Europe. For example, food cooked or touched by a member of a lower caste was thought to be unclean.

Today the caste system is changing rapidly, especially in cities and amongst educated people. The 150 million untouchables are now known as Dalits (the downtrodden). Along with the backward castes they are now an important political force, challenging the power of the upper castes.

Adapted from *Understanding Global Issues*, 97/1

# Historical changes

## Out of the past

**A** Lady Florence Streatfield (seated left) and Sir Benjamin Simpson (standing right) enjoying a Victorian tea party in colonial Calcutta 1890.

### Ancient India

'Modern' India has only existed since independence in 1947. However throughout history India has been influenced by contact with peoples from across Asia and Europe. This has helped to make India such a varied place today. Some key events in the past were:

- 2600–1600BC The Indus Valley civilization built the great cities of Moenjodaro and Harappa in the Punjab.
- 1500BC Around this time the Aryan people invaded India from the North. In southern India a number of empires grew up and collapsed.
- 1500–1700AD The Moghul empires grew up, beginning to make India more like a single country.

- From around 1500AD traders from Europe arrived in India by sea. They were interested in taking India's spices, rice, silk and sugar cane back to Europe.

### The British in India

India's wealth made it very attractive to the British. Britain used force to take over the country and made it a **colony**. Britain gained control in several ways:

- The British army defeated the Indian army in battle.
- The British took control of most of India's trade.
- The British made Indians pay taxes and pay rent to landowners.
- The British set up industries in India.

British rule brought some benefits to India, for example:

- A national railway system was built up to help **export** goods.
- English was introduced across India and although it was foreign, it provided a common language.
- A national education system and civil service was set up.
- Export crops were introduced, such as tea, coffee and indigo – a crop used to make blue dye.

But the British gained most from colonialism at India's expense. For example, factory owners in Britain pressured their government to put a 30 per cent import tax on Indian cloth. This destroyed the cloth industry in India and allowed British factories to export cloth there.

**B** Women workers in Bengal sorting out **indigo**, one of the new crops introduced by the British.

**C** Siraj-ud-Daula was the ruler of Bengal in the 1750's who fought against the British in their attempts to take control of this area.

Robert Clive, head of the East India Company, made a fortune of £250 million. At the same time most Indians suffered great hardships. For example, farmers in Bengal were forced to grow indigo on their land instead of food. As Sarbjit Johal says: 'Although 10 million people died in the Bengal famine (1770), farmers were still forced to pay the land tax.'

These sort of inequalities built up discontent in India. They led the Indian people to struggle for independence. As a result of this pressure the British withdrew from power in India, which became independent in 1947.

## FACTFILE

### Gandhi

Mahatma Gandhi was one of the leading figures in the struggle for Indian independence. After studying law in Britain and fighting for Indian rights in South Africa, he returned to India where he took up the cause of independence from the British. He argued that, '*you have been taught that ...British rule in India is beneficial. Nothing is more false! You cannot escape two facts: first that under the British, India has become the world's poorest country; and second, that it is denied advantages and decencies to which any free country is entitled.*'

Gandhi believed in non-violent resistance (*satyagraha*) to the colonialists, although other people within the independence struggle took up arms against the British. Gandhi encouraged Indians to protest in a variety of ways including not paying taxes to the British or buying British-made goods. As a result he was imprisoned on numerous occasions. He also campaigned against the harsh treatment of low-caste members of Indian society and promoted small-scale craft industries. Because of all these actions he became known as Mahatma or 'great soul'.

# India's climate

## ▶ What is India's climate like?

### India's tropical location

India's location close to the Equator and straddling the Tropic of Cancer means that the sun is overhead for most of the year, so temperatures are high. But there are big differences between north and south India, and between places at different **altitudes**.

> 'Whilst the heat is building up to breaking point in the south, the people of Ladakh (in the north) are still waiting for the snow to melt.'

*Lonely Planet Guide to India*

The Himalayas' altitude means they have large areas of snow and ice. Here the difference between day and night-time temperatures can range from below freezing to 30°C.

### The monsoon

India has a **monsoon** climate – named after the heavy summer rains. There are three broad seasons:

- March–May: hot season. Temperatures can reach 40°C but rainfall is often lower than 10mm a month.

- June–September: monsoon season. Heavy rains are brought by the moist south-west monsoon winds – the rains can last four months. Temperatures drop to around 30°C when the rains start.

- October–February: cool season. Temperatures fall to around 20°C with little rain.

The monsoon rains do not fall evenly from year to year, and there are big differences across India. The wettest areas are the upland areas, especially the Himalayas and Western Ghats. The driest areas are north-west and central India.

India has invested in high-tech satellite technology to help predict the start of the monsoon rains. Alongside this, people's local knowledge is also helpful, using signs like bird migrations and changes in wind direction and speed.

**B** The flooding of the River Ganges, following the monsoon rains, deposits a layer of fertile silt on the fields.

**A** Heavy monsoon rains fall from June to September.

## How does the monsoon affect people's lives?

The monsoon is vitally important to India. Two-thirds of farmers rely on monsoon rainfall to water their crops. Monsoon rains make some of India's rivers rise and flood, leaving fertile silt on the surrounding flood plains. A good monsoon means better crops and more jobs in farming and farm industries. Greater use of irrigation has provided water security for some farmers, but in places too much water has been **extracted** from aquifers, or water bearing rocks, so the **water table** has been lowered. The United Nations has reported that this **ground water** is currently being extracted faster than it is **recharged**.

**D** Table of climate data for Jaisalmer

|  | Max temp (°C) | Rainfall (mm) |
|---|---|---|
| **January** | 24 | 2 |
| **February** | 28 | 1 |
| **March** | 32 | 3 |
| **April** | 38 | 2 |
| **May** | 42 | 5 |
| **June** | 41 | 7 |
| **July** | 38 | 90 |
| **August** | 36 | 86 |
| **September** | 36 | 14 |
| **October** | 36 | 1 |
| **November** | 31 | 5 |
| **December** | 26 | 2 |

**C** Climate graph of Bombay

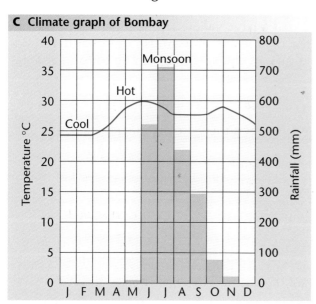

**E** Rainfall map

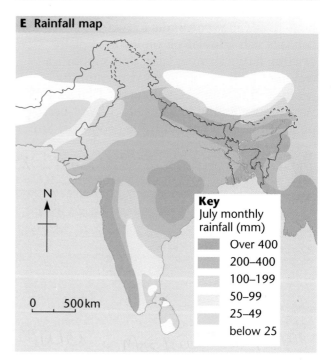

Key
July monthly rainfall (mm)
- Over 400
- 200–400
- 100–199
- 50–99
- 25–49
- below 25

0    500km

### FACTFILE

#### Monsoons and cyclones

*Monsoon* comes from the Arabic *mausin* which means seasonal wind. Over India there are two monsoon winds. In summer south-west winds blow towards low pressue in Central Asia, bringing warm moist air and heavy rain over India. In the autumn, the wind direction changes to north-east. The north-east monsoon is weaker than the summer monsoon, but farmers in east India still rely on it as their main source of water for the year. From October to December the north-east monsoon passes over India, drawing cyclones off the Bay of Bengal.

Cyclones are severe storms which form over tropical oceans, with extremely high winds and heavy rain. The east coast of India is at risk from cyclones, especially the low-lying Ganges delta.

The monsoon and cyclones are both hazards in the region. For example, in April 1990 a cyclone killed 140 000 people in Bangladesh and affected the lives of 12 million. The damage was estimated at $1.8 million. In May around 1 000 people were killed when a cyclone hit Andhra Pradesh in SE India. It affected nearly 9 million people and caused $600 million of damage. In July severe flooding Killed hundreds of people in northern and central India, with more dying in Bangladesh when the Brahmaputra burst its banks.

In April 1991, another severe cyclone hit Bangladesh. A 7m high tidal wave with winds over 200km an hour swept over the coast and delta, killing 125 000 people.

# The Ganges River Basin

## The Ganges Basin

The Ganges is one of the world's longest rivers, flowing over 2500km from its source in the Himalayas to its delta in the Bay of Bengal. This huge river valley cuts India in two. The river deposits rich **alluvial** silt on its flood plain, creating fertile farming land. This supports a region of high population density running north-west to south-east along the Ganges valley. For instance, in the Indian state of West Bengal, population density reaches 766 people per km$^2$.

The Ganges begins high in the Himalayas where it is created by melting snow and ice. Here it is a fast-flowing stream full of white, turbulent water. It flows through steep, narrow valleys, eroding material from the valley floor and sides. By the time it reaches its mouth the Ganges' channel is over 8km wide, meandering across a large valley. The sediment deposited by the river forms silt islands in its channel, known as chars, which join up to form a delta.

**A** This oblique view shows how India's farm land is densely cultivated, right up to the edges of the river banks.

**B** Crowds gather to bathe in the waters of the Ganges in Varanasi

## The River and Religion

The majority of India's population are Hindu, and for them the Ganges is a sacred and holy place. According to ancient Hindu legend, the river once flowed through heaven itself. For devotees of Hinduism the most famous place to visit on the river is Varanasi (Benares). One million people a year come on a pilgrimage here to bathe and cleanse themselves from sin. They throw flowers, money, and food into the waters as a sacrifice. Another tradition is that Hindus scatter the ashes of their dead relatives there. So the river is an important place in the daily worship and activities of the visiting people, and in the customs and traditions surrounding death.

**C** From source to mouth - the course of the Ganges

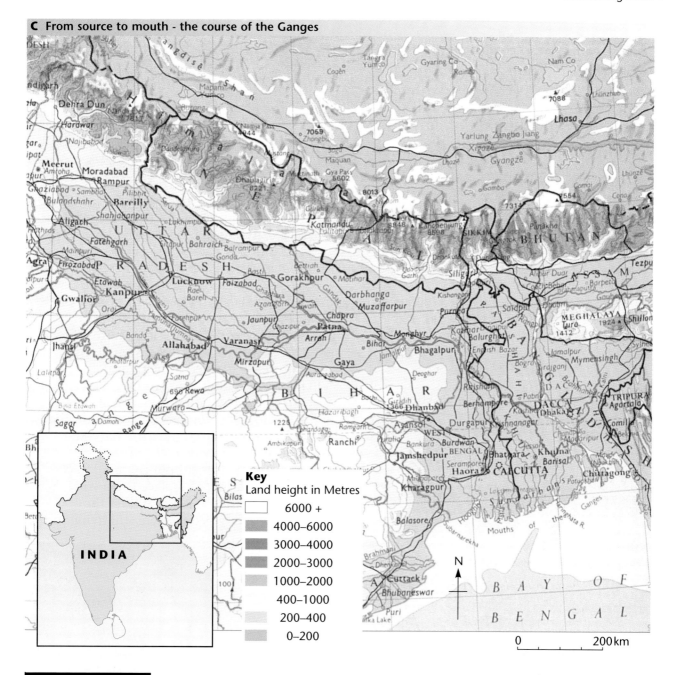

**Key**
Land height in Metres

| | |
|---|---|
| | 6000 + |
| | 4000–6000 |
| | 3000–4000 |
| | 2000–3000 |
| | 1000–2000 |
| | 400–1000 |
| | 200–400 |
| | 0–200 |

N

0        200km

## FACTFILE

### The Ganges River

Length: 2 510km (36th longest in the world and 16th in Asia)
Drainage basin: 980 000 sq km (5th largest in the world)

'In poor and densely populated India, people occupy every inch of space for subsistence and survival. The Ganges river carries millions of tonnes of silt, eroded from the slopes of the Himalayas. For part of the year when flood water recedes, over a million hectares of land become available for cultivation. However, pressure from farming and deforestation over the last century has worsened soil erosion and increased the flood hazard in the Ganges flood plain and its delta.

The Ganges waters are vital to the people living alongside the river. The Ganges is also the home of many endangered species, such as crocodiles. But the river is heavily polluted, partly from the 40 000 people cremated every year at Varanasi, but mainly from industry along its banks, especially in the city of Kanpur.

## Earthquakes

▶ **What is the impact of earthquakes?**

▶ **How do people respond to them?**

### The Latur Earthquake

On the evening of 30 September 1993 the **Latur** region of East Maharashtra, central India, was hit by an **earthquake** measuring 6.4 on the **Richter Scale**. The earthquake completely destroyed over 100 villages, leaving 150 000 people homeless and over 8000 dead. Many organizations came to the aid of earthquake victims, including charities, the Indian army and government.

'Killari village was at the centre. We rushed there, it was beyond imagination. The whole village was destroyed and there were bodies everywhere. We tried to remove the bodies and help people trapped in the debris. Our main aim in the first fifteen days was to give relief to the victims – medical care, food, clothing and shelter.'

Dr Lohiya, from Manavlok, an Indian development charity, describes the earthquake

### Responses to the earthquake

After the earthquake people started to plan for the future. As a local farmer said: 'It was a difficult time, we had nothing. The sowing season had started and we had no seed to plant.'

Paveen Mahajan described the response of Janarth, an Indian development charity: 'We needed to bring people back to normal life. As 90 per cent of the workforce is involved in agriculture we decided to help farmers. Villagers who didn't own land were given loans to help start small enterprises. We also gave fertilizers to richer farmers on condition that the amount was repaid after the harvest.'

The Indian government put up temporary buildings, meaning to replace them with permanent homes. But a year after the earthquake many people were still living in the

**A** The Latur earthquake caused widespread destruction to people's homes and property

**B  Location map of Latur**

Eurasian Plate

Pakistan

Karachi

India

Nepal

Calcutta

Burma

Bombay

Latur
(epicentre)

Bangladesh

Madras

Indian Plate

Sri Lanka

N

0  500km

**C  A collision margin**

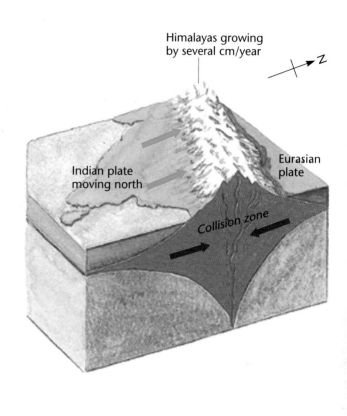

Himalayas growing
by several cm/year

Z

Indian plate
moving north

Eurasian
plate

Collision zone

temporary metal buildings with concrete roofs.
One man said: 'Our old houses were large and
clean. Now we have to live in tiny sheds!'
Many people were also worried about how
dangerous the new buildings would be if
another earthquake struck.

### Why do earthquakes occur in India?

Northern India is an unstable part of the
earth's **crust**. It is close to the boundary
between two **plates**. The Indian Plate is
moving about 5 centimetres northwards each
year towards the Eurasian Plate. Where the two
plates meet is called a **collision plate margin**.

The collision of the two plates has two results.
First, huge pressures build up until the crust
moves suddenly and violently, causing an
earthquake. Second, over millions of years the
pressure has forced the land upwards into **fold
mountains**. These are the Himalayas, the
world's greatest **mountain chain**.

## FACTFILE

### Earthquakes

The strength of earthquakes is measured on the
Richter Scale. This scale ranges from 1 or 2
(which can usually only be measured by special
instruments) up to 9 (where the ground can be
seen to shake and large fissures or gaps open up
in the earth's surface). Each measurement on this
scale marks an increase of a factor of 10. So an
earthquake which reaches 8 on the Richter Scale
is 10 times stronger than an earthquake which
reaches 7.

In the year before the earthquake in Latur 100
tremors were felt in this region. Tremors are
often a sign that an earthquake may occur in the
future. The Latur earthquake reached 6.4 on the
Richter Scale. However the damage was much
greater than that caused by much stronger
earthquakes because the traditional houses in
this area were built from stone. They had little
resistance and many collapsed causing
widespread damage and injuries.

# 2 POPULATION CHANGE AND URBANIZATION

## *Population structure and growth*

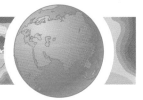

### ▶ How has India's population changed?

### How does India count its population?

> With 900 million people India has the world's second biggest population after China. Every ten years India has a census to count its population. In 1991 '1 500 000 people knocked on every door, crossed inaccessible regions, entered slums, and stooped next to the thousands living on the streets to count India's population.'

*India Year Book*

### Changes in population size

Populations change due to the:
- number of children being born – the **birth rate**
- number of people dying – the **death rate**
- migration – people moving in or out the country.

The difference between the birth and death rates is called the rate of **natural increase**.

**A** A doctor providing family planning advice from a mobile clinic

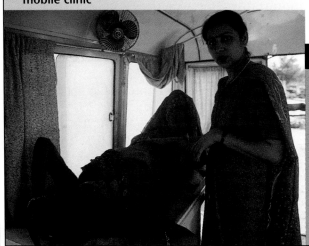

India's population has grown from 236 million in 1891, to 900 million people today. This is because its death rate fell rapidly while its birth rate fell less sharply (figure B). Today the rate of population growth is about 2 per cent.

| B Changes in India's Birth and Death Rates (per 1000 people) | | | | | | | | | | | |
|---|---|---|---|---|---|---|---|---|---|---|---|
| | 1891 | 1901 | 1911 | 1921 | 1931 | 1941 | 1951 | 1961 | 1971 | 1981 | 1991 |
| **Births** | 48 | 46 | 49 | 48 | 47 | 44 | 41 | 42 | 41 | 36 | 30 |
| **Deaths** | 42 | 44 | 43 | 48 | 41 | 31 | 27 | 22 | 19 | 15 | 10 |

Birth rates and death rates can change for a number of reasons, including:
- improved health and sanitation
- natural disasters
- the availability of family planning
- education for girls and women
- changes in the age of marriage
- changes in people's ideas about family size
- changes in people's wealth and standard of living.

### FAMILY PLANNING

During the 1970s India's government tried to reduce population growth by offering people incentives to become sterilized. But many people were forcibly sterilized and this campaign ended in failure. Today India's family planning services are more widely available, and over 40 per cent of Indian women choose to use them. Better education for women and later ages of marriage have also helped slow down population growth.

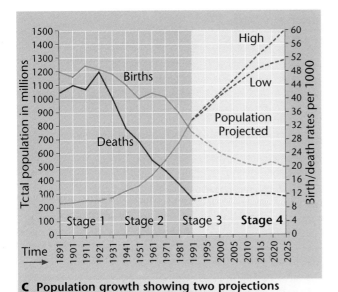

**C Population growth showing two projections**

## What is the impact of population growth?

Population growth creates extra demands for resources, jobs and services. However, it is important to understand why people have larger families. In areas with few health services, parents may need to have five children in order to guarantee that three survive. Children's work can help support the family and they provide security for their parents' old age.

## THE DEMOGRAPHIC TRANSITION

**D Demographic transition model**

This model shows how population changes in a typical country. It helps explain how India's population may change in future.

**Stage 1** High Fluctuating Stage. Birth and death rates are both high, around 35/1000. The population remains stable and low.

**Stage 2** Early Expanding Stage. Birth rates remain high and death rates start to fall, reaching around 20/1000. This leads to rapid population increase.

**Stage 3** Late Expanding Stage. Birth rates fall rapidly, to around 20/1000. Death rates continue to fall to around 15/1000. Population still increases.

**Stage 4** Low Fluctuating Stage. Birth and death rates are low and stable. Population growth slows down.

## FACTFILE

### India's children

'India's population in mid-1996 was probably around 954 million. The most recent population census counted 844 million on March 1, 1991, of whom 438 million were male and 406 female. Population growth is now a little under 2 per cent. The fertility rate in 1992 was four children per family, down from 6.2 children per family in 1965.

Life expectancy at birth increased from 32 years in 1951 to 61 years in 1992 and male life expectancy is now higher than in Russia. India's population is of such extreme diversity - of language, religion, caste and class – that any simple categorization is very misleading.'

*The Economist*, 1997

In India the role of children is very important. With few social services many parents come to rely on the support of their own children in old age. The extended family, where different generations of the same family live together, is very common.

Within poorer communities children may also be a source of additional income for the family. It is estimated that of India's 206 million children, 17 million work. The majority of children work in agriculture and the construction industry. Many thousands work making carpets and also in matchstick factories. Here a nine-year-old girl, one of the 70 000 children who works in the matchstick factories of Tamil Nadu, describes her day:

'The factory bus picks me up at six in the morning to take me to work. In the factory I place the matches on a rack ready to be put in the boxes. I'm one of the fastest workers in the factory which means I get paid more. In the afternoon I pack the matches into boxes. This is a better job because it's not so cramped and my back and neck don't get as sore. By six o'clock the day's almost over and I'll get my pay of eight rupees (20p). I'll spend one rupee on the bus to get home, leaving me seven rupees for the whole day. I've been working in the factory a long time – ever since I was a child.'

# Population and development

## Population structure

Population pyramids can be used to show the balance between men and women and the balance between different age groups. India's population pyramid for 1990 has a wide base, because there is a high proportion of young people. It also has steep sides, because life expectancy is fairly short. The large numbers of children in the graph below show the birth rate is high and the population is growing. As the wide band of children become older they are likely to have children of their own. This is known as a bottom heavy population pyramid. This pattern is common in economically developing countries.

The pyramid for Britain has far fewer children and a greater proportion of older people because of a longer life expectancy and a lower birth rate. This is known as a top heavy population pyramid; it is common in more economically developed countries.

## Population and development

The structure of a country's population has an important influence on a country's opportunities for development. The diversity of India's population presents many challenges, for example:

• high rates of illiteracy
• low status of women
• demands on India's health service
• demands for better employment opportunities, for example India has 3.6 million unemployed university graduates.

### DEPENDENCY RATIO

A country's dependency ratio shows the number of people who are **economically active**, aged between 15–64, compared to people under 15 years old and over 64. However, this figure does not take account of people who are unemployed or children who may be working.

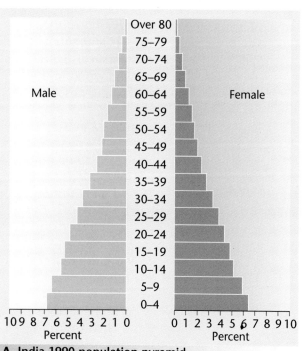

**A** India 1990 population pyramid

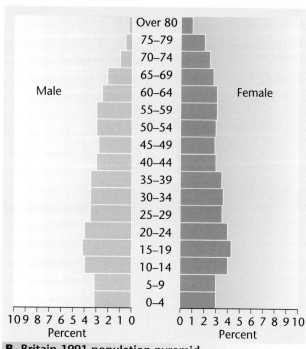

**B** Britain 1991 population pyramid

## India's dependency ratio 1990

$$\frac{\text{Economically inactive (children and old people)} \quad 342\,824\,000}{\text{Economically active (workers)} \quad 503\,381\,000} \times 100 = 68\%*$$

*Britain's dependency ratio in 1990 was 52%

## POPULATION DENSITY

Map **E** shows the distribution of India's population. It shows population density, the average number of people per km$^2$.

| | Male | Female |
|---|---|---|
| **0–9** | 7.5 | 7 |
| **10–19** | 8.5 | 8 |
| **20–29** | 8.5 | 8 |
| **30–39** | 8 | 7.5 |
| **40–49** | 7 | 6.5 |
| **50–59** | 5.5 | 5 |
| **60–69** | 4 | 3.5 |
| **70+** | 2.5 | 3 |

**C** India's population structure in 2025

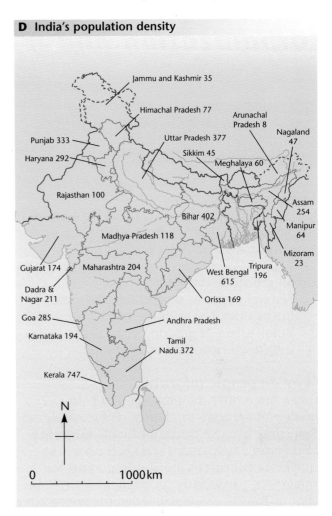

**D** India's population density

## FACTFILE

### Medicine
There are many highly trained doctors in India, but traditional methods of medicine are still often used. After independence there was a renewal of old methods. The Indian traditional system of medicine is known as *Ayuveda* from 'ayus' meaning life and 'veda' meaning knowledge. This method tries to cure disease by studying both mind and body. Most of the medicines are based on herbs, vegetables or animal products. The Hindu god Shiva was the first herbalist and is sometimes drawn carrying herbs in one hand and a lotus flower in the other.

### Yoga
Just as Indian medicine looks at both mind and body when curing disease, the philosophy of Yoga in India works at combining the body, mind and spirit. Yoga demands a long course of training. This includes *Yama* – restraining aggressive and undisciplined behaviour. It insists on no stealing, no lies, no violence, no unnecessary possessions; *Niyama* – restraining one's own body, no anger, no selfishness, resigning oneself to what life brings and *Asanas* – learning certain exercises and postures, some of which are well known in the West.

Yoga also includes training to learn how to control one's breathing and one's senses and how to meditate or control one's own thoughts. Yogis, or men who have practised yoga for many years, are capable of extraordinary feats, such as stopping their own heart beat and starting it again.

# Urbanization and migration

## ▶ Why do people move to India's urban areas?

### Urbanization

India's countryside is home to 74 per cent of the population, but towns and cities are growing at a rate of 3 per cent a year.

Urban growth is caused by:
1. Natural Increase, when there are more births than deaths in the city.
2. Rural–urban Migration, when people move into towns from the countryside.

### Why do people migrate?

Cities often offer the prospect of a better quality of life than rural areas. For example, in Bangalore over 52 per cent of male **migrants** said better employment was their reason to move. Social reasons are also important for migration, particularly for women, with 75 per cent of Bangalore's female migrants saying they moved because of family responsibilities.

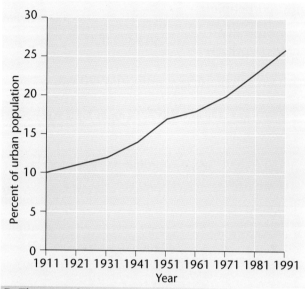

**B** The growth in % urban population

### Where do the migrants live?

While many migrants move to good accommodation, others end up living in shanty towns and slums. Here migrants often build the houses themselves out of wood and other materials, usually on waste land, such as alongside railway lines or roadsides. Because these areas are unplanned, they are often known as **informal settlements**. They usually have few amenities, and few opportunities of the city providing them with any.

Although these settlements look ramshackle they contain a wide range of small-scale industries and services.

**A** The city of Ahmedabad where shanty settlements have been set up in areas of unused waste land.

**C** Quality of life: urban–rural contrasts

| | Urban | Rural |
|---|---|---|
| **Access to proper sanitation** | 50% | 2.5% |
| **% living in poverty** | 20% | 33% |
| **Infant Mortality Rate (IMR)** | 50/1000 | 86/1000 |
| **Total household assets (in Rupees)** | Ru 41 000 | Ru 36 000 |
| **% living within 1km of doctor** | 47% | 20% |

**D Reasons for migration**

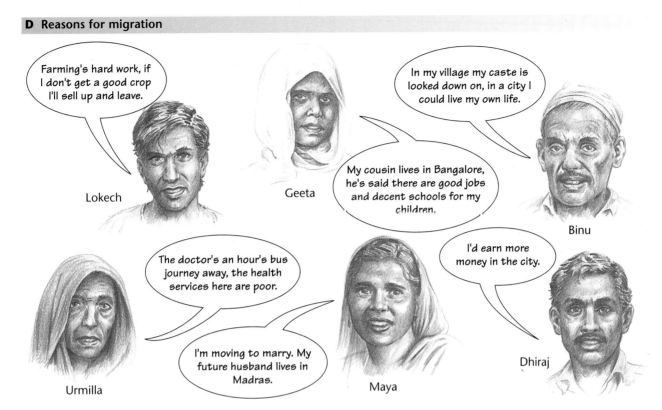

Lokech: Farming's hard work, if I don't get a good crop I'll sell up and leave.

Geeta

Binu: In my village my caste is looked down on, in a city I could live my own life.

My cousin lives in Bangalore, he's said there are good jobs and decent schools for my children.

Urmilla: The doctor's an hour's bus journey away, the health services here are poor.

Maya: I'm moving to marry. My future husband lives in Madras.

Dhiraj: I'd earn more money in the city.

Problems of informal settlements are:
- Lack of sanitation, water and electricity.
- High living densities, families living in single rooms.
- Some cities try to clear informal settlements by bulldozing them. Many shanty towns are liable to flood or are built next to rubbish dumps.

Informal settlements provide:
- Cheap accommodation which people can build themselves.
- Employment opportunities.
- A first foothold in the city.

## Other migrations in India

Migration has not only occurred from rural to urban areas. One of the largest migrations in India was at independence when the country was partitioned, that is, divided into India and Pakistan. During this period 15 million people migrated between these two countries. Many Indians have also migrated further afield to Europe, North America, Eastern Africa, the Caribbean and the Middle East. Money sent back to India from these migrants brings $5 billion into the Indian economy.

## FACTFILE

**Differences between rural and urban India**

|  | Rural | Urban |
|---|---|---|
| Average age of marriage for girls | 16.5 | 17.5 |
| Population growth rate 1981-91 | 3.1% | 1.8% |
| Number of households | 94 million | 29 million |
| Birth rate/1000 (1990) | 32 | 25 |
| Death rate/1000 (1990) | 11 | 7 |
| Use of electricity for lighting | 15% | 64% |

21

# Life in India's cities

**Delhi bans Smokers as Pollution Solution**
'Delhi has banned public smoking to clean up its foul air. Delhi is the world's most polluted city, with 7500 people dying from respiratory illnesses caused by vehicle emission and industrial smog.'

*The Sunday Telegraph*

## India's urban areas

India's cities provide many scenes which would not seem out of place in a city from an economically developed country, such as high-rise flats, industrial developments, bustling shops, traffic-filled roads and busy offices. However, alongside these are also the shanty developments and informal economy that are a feature of high rural–urban migration.

One problem of urban development is air pollution, caused by the growth of traffic and industry. It is estimated that 40 000 deaths a year are related to India's pollution. This has led to some drastic steps being taken.

Industries have also been responsible for accidents such as the Bhopal disaster in 1984, when a cloud of poisonous gas escaped from the Union Carbide chemical factory in Bhopal. Most of the 15 000 victims lived in areas of slum buildings situated around the edge of the factory. In 1997 claims for compensation from the American owners were still continuing.

Urban areas are the main locations for India's industrial development because they need facilities – such as power and good communications as well as employees. This has helped create an **urban bias**, with a wide divide growing up between rural and urban areas. For example, urban wages rates are three times those in rural areas.

**A** The Hiranandani complex is just one of Mumbai's (Bombay's) growing number of expensive housing developments.

**B** Tenement housing provides accommodation for much of Mumbai's ( Bombay's) population.

Urbanization has led to the expansion of cities into rural areas through **peri–urban growth**. This is where new settlements develop on the edges of cities. The settlement of Anand Gram, located 15km from central Delhi, is an example of this type of growth. The settlement was started on an uninhabited part of a flood plain, today 200 people live there. People work in both farming, for example rearing animals, and urban jobs such as printing. The community has improved the area by providing a well, electricity, sanitation, brick buildings and a training centre.

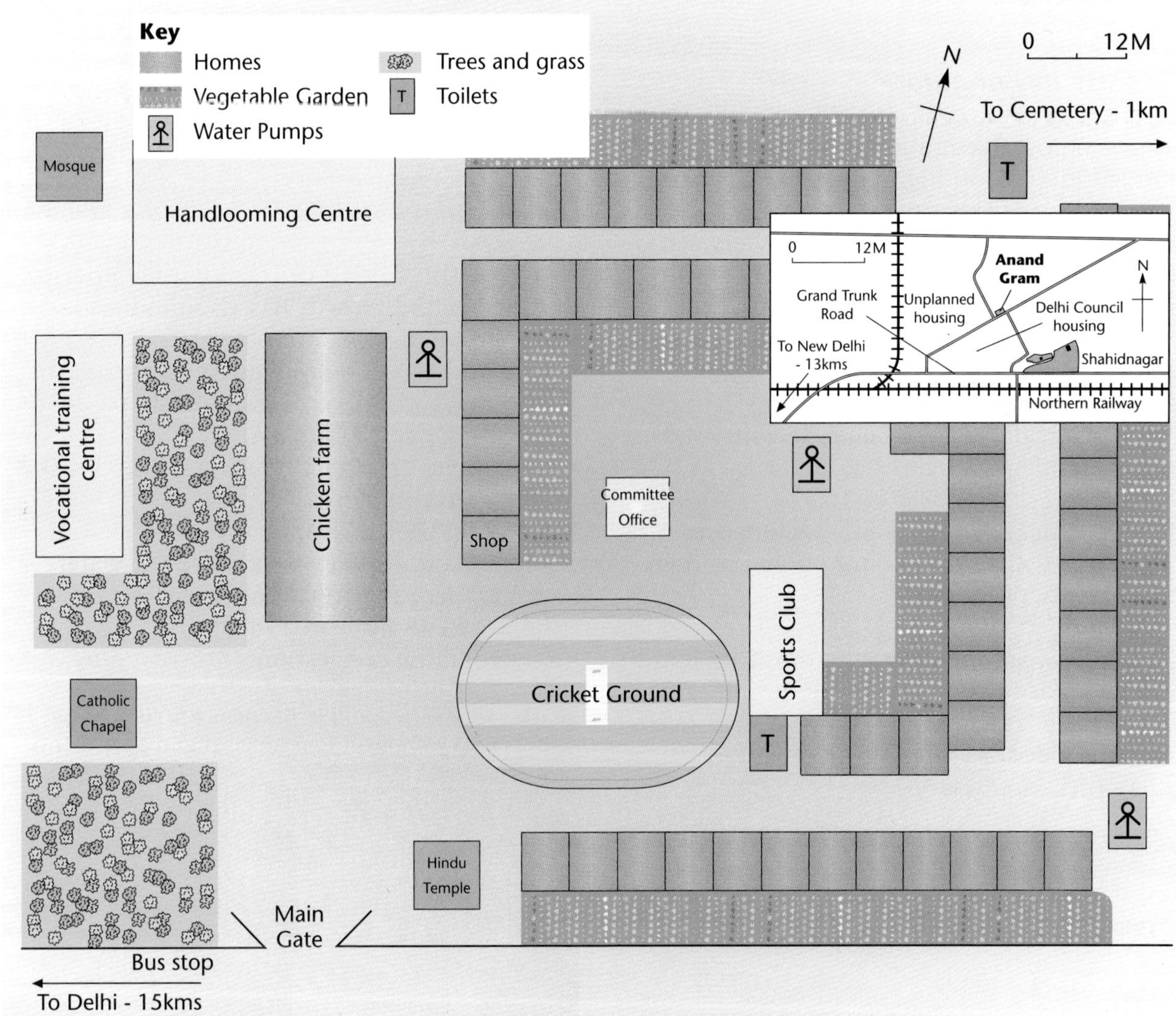
Key
Homes
Vegetable Garden
Water Pumps
Trees and grass
Toilets
N
0 12M
To Cemetery - 1km
Mosque
Handlooming Centre
Anand Gram
Grand Trunk Road
Unplanned housing
Delhi Council housing
To New Delhi - 13kms
Shahidnagar
Northern Railway
Vocational training centre
Chicken farm
Shop
Committee Office
Sports Club
Cricket Ground
Catholic Chapel
Hindu Temple
Main Gate
Bus stop
To Delhi - 15kms

**C Location map of Anand Gram**

## FACT FILE

### Shanty towns

Bombay has now been renamed Mumbai.

*'High-rise or Hovel – It's all hot property'*

For sale: one-roomed shanty in Bombay's Mahim Creek slum. No electricity, no running water, no view – except of children splashing in an open sewer. Price £11 000. Whether you are searching for a hovel or for a high-rise Bombay has become the third most expensive city in the world. Bombay probably has more millionaires than London, but many middle-class Indians – a teacher say earning £150 a month – cannot afford the expensive rents. Many are forced to move to satellite suburbs a two-hour train ride away. Bombay's port, which handles half of India's foreign trade and its factories generating more than 30 per cent of Gross Domestic Product exerts a strong pull on Indians in the countryside, desperate for work.

*The Independent*, 19 March 1995

# Bangalore

## ▶ What is life like in Bangalore?

### Diversity in Bangalore

Bangalore is the capital city of Karnataka state – it has almost five million inhabitants. It was founded in 1537 on high ground 1000 metres above sea level. This gave a good defensive position to control the trade routes between Mysore and Madras. Bangalore became an important fortress, particularly during the 1800s when Tipu Sultan defended this area against the British colonists. Following his defeat the British expanded the city – its altitude provided a cooler climate which was more bearable for them.

Modern Bangalore is a clean, spacious and well-planned city. It was once known as the 'Garden City of India'.

Bangalore is rapidly advancing towards Nehru's vision of it as India's 'City of the future'. It's name in the language of Karnataka state means 'town of boiled beans'. Bangalore is now India's fifth-largest city.

| Year | No. of people |
|------|---------------|
| 1941 | 411 000 |
| 1951 | 786 000 |
| 1961 | 1 203 000 |
| 1971 | 1 664 000 |
| 1981 | 2 922 000 |
| 1991 | 4 087 000 |
| 1996 (est.) | 5 000 000 |

**A** Population growth in Bangalore

### Life styles in Bangalore

As with all Indian cities there is a wide range of lifestyles here. Bangalore is one of India's boom towns with the growth of many electronics factories. This has created considerable wealth.

'It is said that Bangalore is the fastest growing city in Asia, and definitely India's yuppie heaven.'

*Lonely Planet Guide*

However, this wealth exists alongside poverty. The city's rapid growth has also produced many problems. These include:

- High level of unemployment. Low paid informal jobs like collecting waste paper for recycling pays 20 Rupees/day.
- A shortage of proper housing – over 500 000 people live in slums.
- Stress on the city's amenities such as water supply and sanitation. In 1941 the water supply per person per day was 99 litres, falling to 45 litres in 1988.
- Severe traffic congestion.

**B** This shanty building in Bangalore is soon to be replaced with luxury penthouses and apartments.

## Land use in Bangalore

The city centre has developed as two areas around the historic hill fort and British cantonment. Today central Bangalore forms a crescent area of businesses, shops and offices. This is known as the central business district (**CBD**). To the west, south and south-east the CBD is encircled by a wide area of lower-cost housing. This pattern is broken in the north and north-east where a sector of high-cost housing reaches out to the outskirts. To the north-west factories have grown up on an area of flat land alongside major road and rail links. Areas of slum building are scattered across the city, although they are mainly located at the outskirts or alongside main roads and railways, where people can occupy the land.

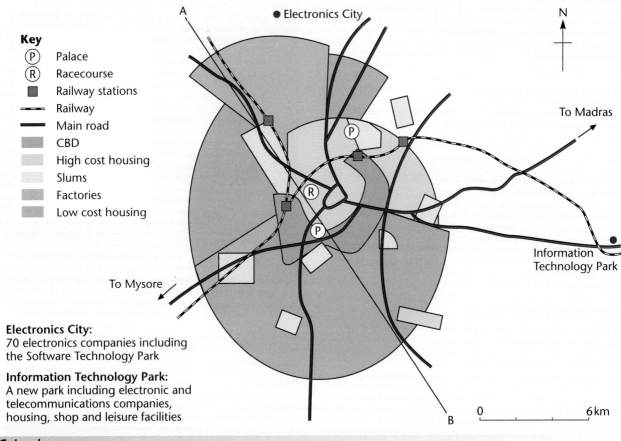

**Key**
- (P) Palace
- (R) Racecourse
- ■ Railway stations
- ═══ Railway
- ─── Main road
- CBD
- High cost housing
- Slums
- Factories
- Low cost housing

**Electronics City:**
70 electronics companies including the Software Technology Park

**Information Technology Park:**
A new park including electronic and telecommunications companies, housing, shop and leisure facilities

**C  Land-use map**

---

## FACTFILE

### Industrial planning in Bangalore

Karnataka state's industrial policy has helped economic growth in Bangalore. The city has eleven industrial areas between 14 and 40km from the city, with more planned. The state buys and develops the land, putting in services such as water, power and telephone links and industrial units.

**Electronics City** was established in 1978. It is the largest concentration of electronics companies in Bangalore, including Motorola (making pagers) and Hewlett Packard (computers). Nearby, Electronics City 2 is just opening up.

**Information Technology Park** was begun in 1995 and is due to be completed in 1999, costing US $300 million to build. Nearby an **Exports Promotion Park** is due to open in 1998, close to the airport and inland container terminal. It will contain non-polluting industries such as electronics, software, clothing and machine tools.

Bangalore's plan to build industrial estates outside the city has some disadvantages. Many employees have to commute by bus from the city over poor roads. There are also problems with water and electricity supply. In the long term, these industrial estates may just speed up the outward spread of the city.

# 3 RURAL DEVELOPMENT

## Rural India

> ▶ **What types of farming are found in India?**

**A** New agricultural machinery being used to plough fields in Gujarat.

### India's countryside

India is sometimes described as a nation of 800 000 villages. Over 60 per cent of India's people work in the countryside. Examples of people's work include the pastoralists of the Himalayan foothills, and the wheat farmers of the Punjab, whilst the countryside includes the paddy fields of Bengal and the tea estates of the Nilgiri Hills. Although most people in the countryside work in agriculture, there are also other activities such as forestry, mining, small-scale manufacturing and services.

### The Monsoon

Because only 30 per cent of India's farms are irrigated, rural life is closely connected to the monsoon, especially its rainfall pattern. The monsoon produces three farming seasons during the year: the hot season, the monsoon season and the cool season (see page 10).

Farmers in states such as Karnataka, Maharashtra, Orissa, Tamil Nadu and Madhya Pradesh rely greatly on the monsoon rains. Here a 1 per cent drop in rainfall can lead to a 0.5 per cent drop in harvests. In the Punjab, Haryana, Kerala, Assam and Andrha Pradesh irrigation and scientific farming means that farmers no longer depend totally on the monsoon.

### Farming types

Many of India's farms are small scale and run by families. These farms often grow food crops, such as rice, wheat, pulses and vegetables, which will be eaten by the family themselves. Extra crops are also gown that are sold to earn money. These farms are often only a few hectares in size and use low levels of technology and small levels of **pesticides** and **fertilizers**.

Commercial farms grow cash crops, including sugar, tea, coffee, spices, cotton, rice and wheat to be sold. Commercial farms are often large, and employ labourers to work the land. These farms also use mechanization, pesticides and fertilizers. Investing in these technologies is expensive, so family farms are often less likely to grow cash crops. Jobs on commercial farms provide employment for the 30 per cent of Indian rural families who do not have enough land to support themselves.

|  | 1980 | 1995 |
|---|---|---|
| **Sugar** | 129 | 285 |
| **Cotton** | 7.0 | 9.4 |
| **Rice** | 53.6 | 80 |
| **Wheat** | 36.3 | 65.2 |

(millions tonnes EIU reference)

**B** Agricultural production [*The Economist*]

# PLANTATIONS

The British forced Indians to grow cash crops such as cotton, jute, indigo, coffee, tea and sugar, for export back to Britain. These were often grown in large British-owned estates called **plantations**. Plantations covered many thousands of hectares and often reduced the land available for food crops. The importance of these crops continues today, with tea production reaching almost 800 million kilograms of which 185 million kilograms is exported.

**C** Farmers transplanting rice in paddy fields in Kashmir.

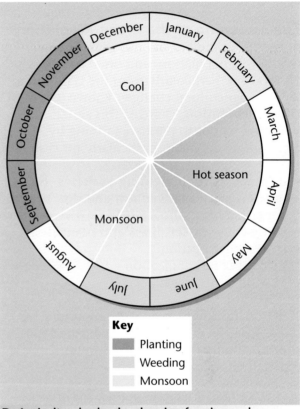

**Key**
- Planting
- Weeding
- Monsoon

**D** Agricultural calendar showing farming cycle

# FACTFILE

### Diet

Many Indian meals begin with a starter. This could be a selection of chutneys and vegetables with spicy sauces. It is usually served with *poppadoms* (large spiced crisps). Meat, chicken or vegetables are served with rice as a main course. They are often eaten with *chapattis* – a type of bread pancake which can be used to scoop up the food. Spices such as chilli, cumin, cinnamon, coriander and ginger are used in many Indian dishes. The meal is often finished off with fresh fruit or a sweet dish. *Kulfi*, a type of ice cream, is popular in hot weather. In rural India people usually sit on the floor or on small wooden stools to eat. The food is often served on a sheet or tablecloth on the floor.

Food varies from region to region. In northern India, where curries tend to be quite hot, they eat dried beans and lentils (dal) a lot, Tandoori food (meat, chicken and naan bread cooked in a *tandoor* – a dome-shaped charcoal oven) and Basmati rice which is grown on the northern plains.

In the west near the coast there is more fish and the food is milder. The hottest curry of them all, Madras curry, comes from the south. In the east, Bengal is famous for its sweets, for example *jelabis* which are first deep fried and then soaked in sweet red syrup.

# The Green Revolution

## How is agriculture changing in India?

### The beginning of the Green Revolution

In the 1950s India could not grow enough food for its population, and often had to rely on food aid, particularly from the USA. But a series of agricultural changes, known as the **Green Revolution**, changed this situation. Scientists set out to improve farming by increasing crop yields, particularly for cash crops. The changes included:

- Introducing **high yielding varieties** (HYVs) of crops, particularly wheat and rice, to give better harvests.
- Using chemical fertilizers and pesticides.
- Increasing irrigation.
- Increasing mechanization.
- Making farms bigger.

These changes have been very important for India. By 1990, India had moved from food shortages to producing a food surplus, especially in rice and wheat.

**India to be Third Biggest Rice Exporter**

'India, which struggled to achieve self-sufficiency, will become the world's third largest rice exporter (after USA and Thailand). Aided by eight good monsoons, and easier exports, India exported 900000 tonnes of rice in 1994/5.'

*Financial Times*

### The Green Revolution in the Punjab

Conditions in the Punjab were ideal for the Green Revolution. The Punjab is located in the north-west of India, an area with many rivers and irrigation canals. Over 80 per cent of its land is suitable for agriculture, compared to the Indian average of 50 per cent, and much is irrigated. Farming in the Punjab is so successful that although it only makes up 1.5 per cent of India's land area, the Punjab accounts for 11 per cent of its agricultural production.

**A** The patchwork landscape of fields and irrigation channels in an intensively farmed area of Ladakh.

**B** In the Punjab the Green Revolution has lead to mechanized farming, including the use of combine harvesters.

## C  The Green Revolution at village level

|  | 1955 | 1965 | 1978 | 1986 |
|---|---|---|---|---|
| % of crops land irrigated | 60% | 80% | 100% | 100% |
| Mechanization | none | none | four tractors | nine tractors |
| Population | 876 | – | – | 1076 |
| Average size of farms | 1.97ha | – | 2.31ha | – |
| Weed control | Hoeing and ploughing used to control weeds | | | Herbicides used to control weeds |
| Wage labour rates | 300% increase in incomes from 1965–78 | | | |
| Land prices | 5-fold increase from 1965–78 | | | |
| **Cropping as % of cropped area** | | | | |
| **Summer crops** | | | | |
| maize | 21 | – | – | 40 |
| rice | 0 | – | – | 10 |
| **winter crops** | | | | |
| wheat | 21 | – | – | 69 |
| fodder | 10 | – | – | 1 |
| chick peas | 6 | – | – | 1 |
| Fertilizer | Increase by 300% between 1955 and 1986 | | | |
| **Increase in crop yeilds** | | | | |
| Wheat (tones/ha) | 1.24 | – | – | 2.73 |
| Rice (tones/ha) | 1.00 | – | – | 2.55 |

## Problems of the Green Revolution

Despite the increased harvests there have been problems created by the Green Revolution. Because new seeds, fertilizers and technology cost money, many poorer farmers have not gained from these changes. As farms have got bigger, more small farmers have become landless and unable to grow food for their families. Instead they often work for larger farmers. The use of pesticides has also polluted some water supplies and the increasing use of water for irrigation has lowered the **water table** in many places, making it more difficult to get at the water from underground.

**D** Increased harvests were based on the introduction of High Yield Variety (HYV) seeds. These required careful attention, including the use of pesticides and artificial fertilisers.

## FACTFILE

### The effects of the Green Revolution

| Indian crops, 1994-95 | |
|---|---|
| Rice | 81 100 000 tonnes |
| Wheat | 65 500 000 tonnes |
| Millet, sorghum and maize | 30 400 000 tonnes |
| Pulses | 14 100 000 tonnes |
| Tea | 737 000 tonnes |
| Coffee | 108 000 tonnes |
| Cotton | 12 100 000 (bales) |
| Jute | 9 500 000 (bales) |
| Sugar cane | 271 000 000 tonnes |

*The Economist, 1997*

**Population growth, food production and consumption in India, 1980-95**

| Year | 1980 | 1990 | 1995 |
|---|---|---|---|
| Population (millions) | 689 | 827 | 931 |
| Food consumption (kcals/person/day) | 1959 | 2297 | 2395 |
| Food production (per person 1980 = 100) | 100 | 116 | 120 |

# Agricultural development in the Thar Desert

## ▶ How is the desert made green?

> 'I have a dream of seeing these great deserts where hardly anything grows converted into fertile lands.'

Kanwar Sain, chief engineer of the Indira Gandhi Canal

### Geographical background

The Thar Desert is a harsh environment. It receives less than 300mm rainfall a year and has poor soils. Life is tough for local people, with poor health, poor education, high infant mortality and female literacy as low as 2 per cent.

### Traditional farming

Traditional farmers in the Thar Desert keep herds of sheep, cattle, goats and camels. They graze over large areas, often with long **migrations**, to find pasture. Everyone shares grazing rights to **common land** – which nobody owns. Only small areas have enough water to grow 'drought resistant' crops like **sorghum**.

### Change in the Thar Desert

Work started on building the Indira Gandhi Canal in 1957. The project has already brought water to 0.5 million hectares at a cost of over $1 billion. It has brought big changes to local farmers, including:

- More irrigated land.
- Richer farmers now irrigate their land for crops, rather than graze animals.
- More cash crops such as chillies and mustard.
- More jobs working in the fields alongside the canal.
- More mechanization (for example, tractors) are used three times more than before.

These changes have also lead to some problems:

- Some richer farmers have taken over common land, replacing grazing land with private fields.
- The soil in many areas has lost its fertility through salination. When irrigation water dries salt is left behind.
- Many local soils have become **eroded** because they are unsuitable for crops.
- Cash crops are thirsty so water supplies are reduced. Chillies need sixteen times more water than sorghum.
- Hollows in the desert have become water logged. Some people now fish in the middle of the desert!
- Many poorer farmers do not have enough money to take advantage of the new changes.

A Pastoralists in Rajasthan herd sheep, cattle, goats and camels over large distances to find water and pasture.

## DEVELOPMENT IN THE THAR DESERT

The URMUL Trust, an Indian non-governmental organization (NGO), works with 60 000 people in the Thar desert. It identified four reasons for poverty:

- Indebtedness.
- Ill health.
- The growth of private fields instead of common land.
- Richer farmers claiming water and land rights from poorer people.

URMUL acted to try and overcome these problems by:

- Providing loans.
- Supporting village health workers.
- Protecting areas of common land.
- Supporting the community's fight for better water and land rights.

The canal has accounted for much of Rajasthan's agricultural expenditure leaving few resources for other small-scale investments in farming.

**B** The water from the major canals of the Indira Gandhi scheme is distributed to smaller canals where electric pumps can irrigate the farmer's fields.

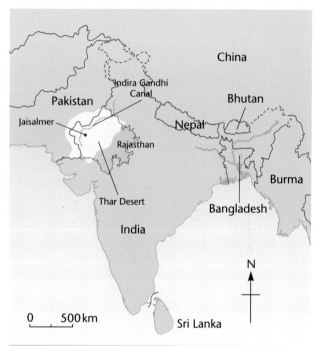

**C** Location map of Thar Desert

## FACTFILE

**The Thar Desert**

There is a plan to extend the canal but URMUL believe that priority must be given to the poor if they are to benefit at all:

'The Indira Gandhi Canal Project must be one of the greatest human engineering achievements. However, we must ask ourselves what can be done to make the project more meaningful to the largest number of people? All the issues URMUL raise address the immediate problems of water-logging and settlement. In a sense these are only symptoms – the real problem is in the lack of a people's voice in planning and decision making. Poorer farmers are drawn into a vicious cycle of mounting debts as they struggle to develop less favourable plots of land. It is so important to give priority to the poor because with the loss of land, they suffer more than the loss of a resource, or money; it is part of the social fabric of existence.'

*URMUL Trust report on Indira Gandhi Canal*

## ▶ How do small-scale farmers make a living?

**A** Farmers in Karnataka state carrying the rice harvest back to their village.

### Family farms

The Nilgiri Hills is one area where many people rely on small-scale farming for their livelihood. Most farmers in this area have very small plots of land, often less than 1.5 hectares in size. On this they grow a wide range of food crops such as rice, bananas, potatoes, onions and vegetables.

These crops are mainly grown to be eaten by the farmers' families but some will be sold for extra cash. Animals are an expensive investment and most of the farmers can only afford to keep a few chickens, possibly a pig or a cow. Almost all the **farm labour** is provided by the family, although people also do work for richer farmers who mainly grow cash crops.

### Cash crops

Cash crops, such as tea, coffee and ginger, are often grown by richer farmers who can afford to buy pesticides, seed and fertilizer. It is often difficult for small farmers to grow cash crops because they cannot afford these inputs or dare not risk a crop failure.

Here is a breakdown for ginger production costs:
- Cost of renting a field £10 (a season, which is about one year)
- Cost of buying pesticides and hiring workers to plant and harvest the field: £312
- Income from selling the crop of ginger: £2083.

## FAMILY FARMS

| Inputs | | Outputs | |
|---|---|---|---|
| **Land:** | small plots less than 1.5 hectares, often owned by the family | **Crops:** | wide range of food crops grown, mainly for family consumption |
| **Labour:** | family | **Animals:** | milk, meat from small animals, eggs. |
| **Technology:** | low levels mainly hand tools or animal plough, little use of pesticides or fertilizers | **Labour:** | some family members may work on richer farmers' land |
| **Crops:** | wide range of different food crops grown from seeds etc. | **Income:** | small income for family from sale of surplus food crops, some income from paid work |
| **Animals:** | manure for fertilizer, used for ploughing | | |

The richer farmers own land or can afford to rent larger fields, so they can get a bigger harvest and a larger income.

They also have enough money to buy more farm animals, which they can raise for sale.

They also provide jobs for small-scale farmers, such as hoeing the land and harvesting ginger and tea. But pay is often little more than £1.00 a day and this work is only available during eight months of the year.

**B** Excess food crops are often sold in local markets, such as this one in the village of Chembakolli in Tamil Nadu.

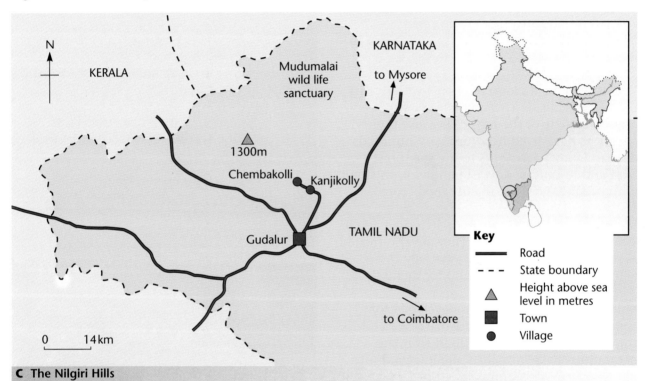

**C  The Nilgiri Hills**

## FACTFILE

### The Nilgiri Hills

The Nilgiri Hills (Blue Hills) stretch over an area of 2540 square km in the state of Tamil Nadu in the south of India. The region has an equatorial climate and its natural vegetation is tropical rainforest. 700 000 people live in the Nilgiri Hills and 80 per cent are small-scale farmers. Tea and coffee plantations take up more than 50 per cent of the cultivated land.

The clearance of the land for plantations has not only affected the population of small-scale farmers in the Nilgiri hills, it has also removed the forests which supported much of this area's wildlife. This area is home to wildlife such as deer, monkeys and a wide range of birds.

One other animal common to this area is the elephant, which are kept by people to help with logging.

The Nilgiri Hills are quite high (2308m). Hill stations were developed as refuges from the heat in British colonial times. Ootacamund, 'the Queen of the Hill Stations' in the Nilgiri Hills, is a popular tourist destination. Ootacamund is the name given by the British to Udhagamandalam. It is popularly referred to as 'Ooty'.

# Tea plantations

## ▶ What has been the impact of the growth of cash crops?

### Tea – a cash crop

The hot, moist conditions in the Nilgiri Hills of southern India support a tropical rainforest ecosystem. The area has a wide variety of climates and vegetation that is very special in India.

The Adivasi are a group of people who live in the Nilgiri Hills. Their name means 'the original people of the forest'. Because their ancestors have lived here for many hundreds of years, they have rights to use the forest's land and resources. Adivasi families farm small plots of land, growing mainly food crops.

Many Adivasi families are poor, living on about 200 Rupees (£4.00) a week. They are also treated as inferiors by other people, especially those who want to farm Adivasi land for themselves.

Much of the forest has been developed for commercial agriculture, particularly tea and coffee plantations. In the Nilgiri Hills the plantations have brought some low-paid jobs into the area. As Padmini says 'I pick tea with my mother, for picking 25 kilos in a day I get 25 Rupees (50p).' But plantations have also produced conflicts over the use of land.

**A** The introduction of tea and coffee plantations resulted in a major change in the land use of the Nilgiri Hills.

## PLANTATION AGRICULTURE

The plantations bring both positive and negative changes.

**Positive:**

- The crops are sold to consumers in India and overseas.
- Tea bushes have to be picked every fifteen days, providing tea picking jobs.
- Workers are needed to transport, process and pack the crops.

**Negative:**

- The plantations reduce the land available to the Adivasi.
- Tea picking is a poorly paid job.
- Workers often have poor job-security and conditions.

**B** The Adivasis people of the Nilgiri Hills demonstrating in support of their rights to land.

To overcome the problem of losing their land the Adivasi, helped by ACCORD a local charity, employed land-rights lawyers to represent them in court. Their land was mapped, so no one else could claim it, and they held a peaceful demonstration of 30 000 people. This showed that they would not allow their land rights to be easily overturned. Chandran says 'Everyone was told about our land-rights and that we shouldn't fear people who threatened us. We all worked together, and now we've enough land and our spirit has returned.'

**C  Land-use map**

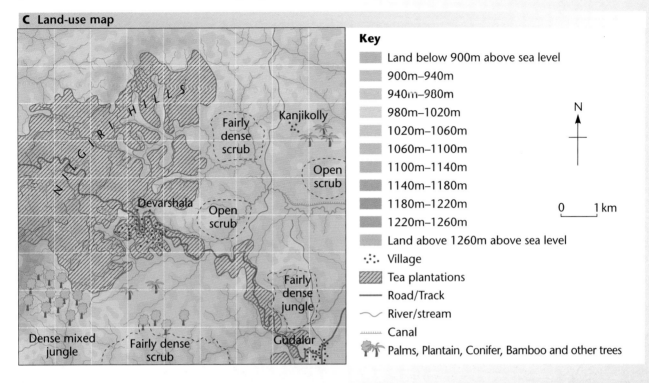

**Key**
- Land below 900m above sea level
- 900m–940m
- 940m–980m
- 980m–1020m
- 1020m–1060m
- 1060m–1100m
- 1100m–1140m
- 1140m–1180m
- 1180m–1220m
- 1220m–1260m
- Land above 1260m above sea level
- ·:·. Village
- Tea plantations
- Road/Track
- River/stream
- Canal
- Palms, Plantain, Conifer, Bamboo and other trees

N

0    1 km

## FACTFILE

### The Adivasi people

Most of the Adivasi people in the Nilgiri Hills live in either thatched or tiled houses in small villages. There are small local shops and tea houses in many of the villages, although Chandran, from Kanjikolly village, has to take the bus to the nearest town of Gudalur for any larger shops and services. Although it is only 14km from Chandran's house to Gudalur the road is in poor condition and very winding and the journey takes about one hour.

The Adivasi people in Chandran's village belong to three different groups, the Paniya, the Bettakurumba and the Kattunaicken. As well as their own group's dialect, people in this area usually also speak Malaylam and Tamil, the state language. The Adivasi people have their own religious ceremonies where they pray to the spirits of the natural world around them – the trees, the sky, the plants, water, rocks and earth, and animals.

**D  Growth of commercial farming in the Nilgiri Hills**

| Year | Area in Hectares |
|------|------------------|
| 1847 | 6164 |
| 1951 | 45694 |
| 1991 | 71921 |

Chandran from Kankikolly village says: 'The main problem here has always been no land for the Adivasis. We've always had to fight the landlords and forestry people. Then the NGO [Non Government Organization] came and told everyone in the village what our rights were and what we could do to get our land.  Now we celebrate the day when all the Adivasis of this area came together to protect our land.'

'I'm happy my family is living here because we are all working together to make life better. We hope the youngsters will have many opportunities to do well and also be proud of being Adivasi.'

# 4 DEVELOPMENT AND ECONOMIC GROWTH

## Development in India

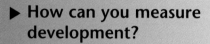

### ▶ How can you measure development?

#### Social and economic development
One of the issues facing India is whether it can provide a good quality of life for all its people. India has the world's largest concentration of poor people, with one-third living in poverty, so investigating Indian development provides important lessons for other countries.

#### Measuring development
There are two main ways to measure development, through investigating the economy and society.

#### The economy
A country's Gross National Product (GNP) measures the wealth it creates each year. GNP per capita (per person) measures the average amount of wealth for everyone in the population. This measure is useful because it is easy to compare countries.

### HOW DEVELOPMENT AFFECTS PEOPLE

Here four Indian people talk about how development affects them.

**1** Sampangi says: 'Without this mechanics job, I'd still be rag picking. Now I can walk with the common people and can get married in the future.'
**2** Nivruti Gaekwad took out a loan to buy irrigation pipes. He says: 'For the first time in my life I've harvested millet in the dry season.'
**3** Thippamma, a health worker, says: 'Before I started, if there were complications with a birth, the mother had to be taken by bullock cart to the hospital 13km away.'
**4** Ponnuthi says: 'Whether boys or girls they should study. I'm responsible for my children and they deserve a chance to become educated so they'll have a better future.'

**A** Ranked by GNP/capita
(1994 World Bank Development Report)

| Country | GNP/capita $ |
| --- | --- |
| Kuwait | 19 420 |
| UK | 18 340 |
| South Korea | 8 260 |
| Romania | 1 270 |
| India | 320 |

| Country | Deaths per 1000 live births |
| --- | --- |
| UK | 6 |
| South Korea | 12 |
| Romania | 24 |
| Kuwait | 26 |
| India | 70 |

**B** Ranked by Infant Mortality Rate
(1994 World Bank Development Report)

There are some problems with measuring development using GNP/capita:

- It overlooks inequalities between rich and poor people.
- Some wealth is created but never measured, for example in informal jobs.
- It focuses only on money and ignores people's quality of life.

**C** This bore-hole will provide a clean supply of water to Rani and Binu's village. It reduces the risk of people falling ill from water-borne disease.

## *Social indicators*

Social indicators measure people's quality of life, for example, their life expectancy, levels of health and education. They can also examine environmental quality, equality between men and women and whether a country is democratic with guaranteed human rights. An important measure is Infant Mortality Rate (IMR), which is the number of deaths per 1000 live births. This highlights levels of health care for babies and their mothers, their diet and also levels of education.

Social indicators give a clearer idea of people's quality of life but they can be difficult to work out. They are also average figures, so there can be wide variation between different parts of a country or between different groups of people.

**D** Traders at Mumbai's (Bombay's) stock market keeping up-to-date with movement in the global economy .

## FACTFILE

### Inequality in India

*Unequal access to health care*. Ill health and disease continue largely because of the lack of attention by India's leaders to poverty, illiteracy and lack of housing. Neglect of health is shown by the paltry spending on disease prevention and health care. India's national and state governments spend about 1.3 per cent of national income on health, far less than other Asian countries. This works out at US $2 to $3 per person – not nearly enough to meet basic health needs.

India's rich and powerful have access to world-class health care in the larger cities, some of it provided cheaply at government hospitals. Top politicians can always get treatment in the west at great expense, whereas for an ordinary person a serious illness can mean financial ruin.

Adapted from *The Financial Times*, 8 November 1994

*Women's rights*. India is a country where boys are often more valued than girls. The proportion of females in the population has declined this century and it is now one of the lowest in the world. In 1901 there were 972 females for every 1000 males, but by 1991 there were only 929. A national Action Plan for the Girl Child for 1991-2000 aims to improve female eduction and to eliminate discrimination.

Adapted from *'Understanding Global Issues'*

# India's industries

**A** Steel, along with other heavy industries, was one of the first industries to be nationalized by India's government at independence.

## India's growing industries

India became independent from Britain in 1947. The first Prime Minister, Jawaharlal Nehru, announced that India would 'awake to life and freedom'. Nehru believed that to become a success India had to develop its own industries, which had been destroyed by the British colonists.

During the 1950s the government set up and took control over, or **nationalized**, many **large-scale industries** including iron and steel, engineering, communications and chemicals. The nationalized industries reduced the need to import goods such as steel which were important in India's development. They also created many jobs, for example, Indian state railways employed 1.6 million people.

## India's steel industry

Steel is one of India's important industries, employing almost 400 000 people. India has seven major **integrated iron and steel plants** producing over 18 million tons of steel a year. The aim is to produce 35 million tons by 1999, making India the world's seventh largest producer of steel. One of the concentrations of this industry is in the state of Bihar, with production at Bokaro, Ranchi and Jamshedpur. The advantages of a **location** here include:

- Good rail and road links with major centres such as Calcutta and Patna, Bihar's state capital.
- Good supplies of **raw materials** needed for steel production – Bihar accounts for 40 per cent of India's iron ore production.
- Good energy supplies, with easy access to major coal fields.
- Lots of flat land providing space for large factories.

## New industries

During the 1950–60s new industries set up producing **consumer goods** for sale in India, such as food and drink, household goods and cars. Many of these were joint ventures with foreign firms, for example, manufacturing British cars in India. However, at this time India was not very attractive to foreign business because of strict **tariffs** and **trade barriers**, set up to protect Indian industries from foreign competition.

In the 1960–70s the **Green Revolution** in India's rural areas helped industries making farm equipment and fertilizers to develop.

Since the 1980s the Indian government has reduced its controls over industry, so allowing businesses to set up more easily. Some nationalized industries have been sold off and trade restrictions reduced. This has allowed many international firms to start production in India, producing goods both for the Indian and export markets. These firms have brought new economic growth and jobs.

**B** Mahatma Gandhi spinning cloth by hand.

| Key | | Bihar State | |
|---|---|---|---|
| `- - -` | International boundaries | **Land area** | 173877 km² |
| `———` | State boundaries | **Population** | 86.34 (million) |
| ○ | State capital | **Population density** | 497 per km² |
| • | Towns | **Natural resources (coal)** | with W. Bengal and Orissa, world's 4th largest reserves |
| ⌇ | River | **Coal production** | 1990-91 219.3 million tonnes |
| ┉ | Railway | | |
| ⛏ | Coal | **Steel** | India produced 18.5 million tonnes in 1993 |
| ⊠ | Iron ore | | |
| ◎ | Steel plants | | |

## Alternatives to industrialization

Mahatma Gandhi, one of the leaders of the independence movement, criticized the path of industrial development taken by India. 'How can a country with millions of living machines afford to have machines which will displace the labour of millions?' Gandhi believed development should focus on **small-scale** rural industries which would be relevant to local people's needs, for example, making farm equipment and weaving cloth. This approach is called **appropriate technology**.

**C** Bihar – centre of India's steel production

## FACTFILE

### India's film industry

The Indian film industry is one of the largest in the world with over 700 films being made every year. Around half are produced in Mumbai (Bombay), more than in Hollywood. Because of the size of India's film industry Mumbai is often known as India's 'Hollywood' or 'Bollywood'.

Many Indians go to the cinema regularly, and songs from films enjoy the same popularity as pop songs in the UK. One of India's best-known film directors is Manmonhan Desai. In Mumbai, because of his success, he is called the 'goose that lays the golden eggs'. His films include the

smash hit '*Amar, Akbar, Anthony*'. It follows the lives of three brothers who are separated by accident at birth and brought up by families of different faiths – Hindu, Muslim and Christian. They are finally reunited following a series of comical adventures and coincidences.

Most films are made in the Hindi language though more are being made in regional languages such as Tamil, Bengali and Maharati. Adventure films, romances and films about Indian society are always popular. Some film stars go on to become politicians.

► What is the role of transnational companies in India?
► What advantages and disadvantages do they bring?

## New industrial developments

Since the 1980s many **transnational companies** (TNCs) have set up in India. TNCs are businesses which have offices and factories in many countries – some TNCs are wealthier than small countries. H D Deve Gowda, India's Prime Minister, greeted these changes saying, 'We welcome foreign investment in sectors like power, tourism, ports and **high-tech** industries.'

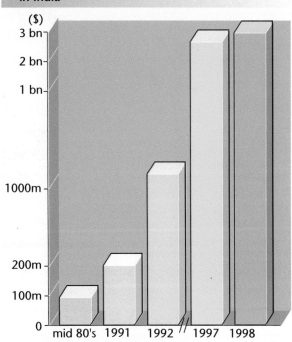

**A  Overseas Investment (from USA, EU and Japan) in India**

Large numbers of overseas firms have set up in India to take advantage of low wages and the growing demand for consumer goods by India's population. They have been helped by fewer government controls over the economy. These industries have brought many benefits to the Indian economy, for example:
• Providing job opportunities.
• Generating tax income for India.
• Creating demand for Indian raw materials and power supplies.

• Creating demand for services and products from Indian firms.
• Bringing new skills and technologies into India.
• Producing goods for sale to India's people as well as internationally.

However, some TNCs bring problems too, for example:
• Low wages.
• Materials may be imported from outside India, reducing the need for materials from Indian suppliers.
• They may pollute the environment.
• **'Tax breaks'** are often offered to encourage the industries to locate in India, reducing the taxes India receives from the companies.
• Because TNCs have their headquarters outside India, usually in the USA, EU or Japan, the companies could relocate to another country at any time.

Many of these industries also produce goods to be sold outside India, for example, sportswear, electronic goods such as radios, and cars. This has led to a changes in the pattern of India's exports as manufactured goods have increased compared to India's traditional exports of agricultural produce.

**B  Bill Gates visiting India, 1997. He is the president of Microsoft, the world's largest software transnational...**

**C** Foreign Investment in India: 1992 (%)

| | |
|---|---|
| USA | 31.7 |
| Switzerland | 17.7 |
| Japan | 15.7 |
| UK | 3.0 |
| Other Europe | 7.8 |
| Indians living abroad | 11.3 |
| Others | 12.8 |

**D** IT transnational companies in India

| | Revenue Rs m. |
|---|---|
| Hewlitt Packard | 5780 |
| IBM | 3560 |
| ACER | 3200 |
| INTEL | 2700 |
| Digital | 2590 |
| Compaq | 2000 |
| Sun | 1700 |
| Microsoft | 1120 |
| Apple | 1100 |
| Citizen | 810 |

**E** Wealth of India and the world's six biggest transnationals, 1994

| | |
|---|---|
| India | 304 (GDP $billion) |
| General Motors | 169 (sales $billion) |
| Ford | 137 |
| Toyota | 111 |
| Exxon | 110 |
| Shell | 110 |
| IBM | 72 |

### Farmers Ransack US Chain in India.

'Nearly 100 farmers broke through a police cordon and ransacked a Kentucky Fried Chicken outlet, demanding that the multinational fast-food leave India.'

*International Herald Tribune*

**F** Not all of the multinational firms have been welcomed by all sections of India's population. Some TNCs have been accused of bringing foreign influences into India, known as 'cultural imperialism', particularly from America.

## FACTFILE

### Transnationals and India's software industry

India has many advantages for transnational companies trying to cut costs. For example in the software industry.

- Programmers in the USA, W. Europe and Japan earn about $4000 a month, but Indian programmers are paid about $800 a month.
- India has 1.4 million software programmers, second only to the number in the USA.
- Indian universities produce large numbers of very well educated graduates.

- When it is night time in North America and Europe, programmers in India can maintain western companies' software systems and process their data, using high speed satellite links.

India's software industry is made up of Indian companies, transnationals like IBM, and **joint ventures** between Indian and overseas companies.

# Economic growth in Bangalore

▶ **How is economic growth affecting Bangalore?**

**A** The development of computer software is one of India's boom industries.

## Bangalore – a boom town

Bangalore, in Karnartaka State, is one of India's boom cities. It has grown over 1000 times since independence. Its economy, based on new computer industries, is growing fast too.

The Economist Intelligence Unit reported that, 'One of India's strong growth areas is computer software, where export turnover rose by 64 per cent in 1995.' The software industry is now worth $1.2 billion (the total IT industry being worth $2.2 billion) and much of its growth is concentrated in Bangalore. Here there are over 300 software businesses, one-third of them owned by multinationals like Hewlett Packard, IBM and Digital.

Today electrical engineering employs over 7 per cent of the total workforce of Bangalore, with 10 000 people working in high-tech businesses.

## So why has Bangalore become so successful?

- Historical tradition: Bangalore has a tradition of high-tech industries. Many government research companies were already located in this area, such as India Telecom Industries, Hindustan Machine Tools and the India Space Research Organization.
- An educated and skilled work force: There are many colleges, universities and research institutes which train people to work in high-tech industries.
- Good communications: Bangalore has an airport and advanced satellite communications. These allow quick communications with firms in Europe and America.
- Government support: The State government has supported high-tech industries by creating business parks and amenities and encouraging businesses.
- Quality of life: The cooler local climate and the large number of parks and green areas give Bangalore its name of 'India's Garden City'. 'Bangalore took off because of the quality of people and the quality of life,' says Namdan Nilakeni, who founded Infosys Technologies, one of Bangalore's largest companies with sales of $28 million.

**B** Alongside jobs and wealth, economic growth has also brought traffic congestion and pollution.

# WHAT BENEFITS HAS GROWTH BROUGHT?

Dilip D'Souza of *New Internationalist* says, 'Software has certainly brought prosperity to thousands of people, but there is a down side too.' Bangalore has grown very quickly so there is a housing shortage. Large numbers of people live in slum dwellings and the city's electricity, water and sewage services struggle to keep up with the pressures placed on them. The airport was designed to cater for 700 people a day and now struggles to cope with 6000 a day. The streets are often congested with Bangalore's 850 000 vehicles. 'City garbage is often uncleared; water is getting scarce; traffic is a nightmare; public transport is hopelessly inadequate and house prices are beyond the reach of ordinary people,' stated Dilip D'Souza.

## C India's computer industry in Bangalore

### Computer Industry

Indias computing industry has grown rapidly over the last 15 years, with Bangalore in Southern India becoming the 'electronics capital' of the country. Many multinational companies have established bases in India. These provide 24-hour a day online software support at a fraction of the cost of paying shift workers in Europe of the USA. Companies which are currently using India for 'offshore' support include Abbey National, North West Water, Reuters and Avis Europe.

In addition, there are over 700 software companies in India, employing more than 140,000 people. Computer hardware and electronic components are also manufactured in India. These firms earn 80 - 90% of their income from exports, but India's internal computer based services remain undeveloped.

India is attractive for foreign computer companies like IBM, Microsoft, Texas Instruments and Compaq because overall costs are about 50% of those in the West: wages especially are lower than those in the USA and Europe, making it cheaper for companies to employ experienced and talented people. However, because reliable electricity supplies and comm-unication networks are often not available locally, hi-tech companies have to provide these facilities themselves, increasing their costs.

Source: *Global Eye*, Issue 4, Autumn 1997

## D Changing employment in Bangalore

| | Electronics % of employees | Textiles % of employees |
|---|---|---|
| 1941 | 0.0 | 12.0 |
| 1951 | 1.0 | 14.6 |
| 1961 | 2.8 | 13.7 |
| 1971 | 6.0 | 10.5 |
| 1981 | 6.8 | 8.0 |
| 1991 | 8.0 | 7.0 |

## FACTFILE

### The IT industry

The IT industry is one of India's success stories. In 1996 the software industry was growing by about 50 per cent a year, with 40 per cent of sales in India and 60 per cent for export. For example, when trains on the London underground run on time, or American Airways planes take off safely, it is partly thanks to software designed in India.

| India's software cities | |
|---|---|
| Mumbai (Bombay) | 34% |
| Bangalore | 26% |
| Delhi | 20% |
| Pune | 6% |
| Calcutta | 5% |
| Others | 9% |

| Software exports 1996 | |
|---|---|
| US | 57% |
| Europe | 22% |
| Asia | 13% |
| Others | 8% |

# Tourism in Goa

▶ **What is the impact of tourism in one area?**
▶ **How do economic changes affect people?**

'Goa is a delightful place beside the Arabian Sea, with golden beaches, gleaming white washed houses and perhaps the friendliest people in India.'

**A** Goa's coastline of white sands and palms provides the ideal location for a beach holiday.

Goa is located on India's western coast. It was once a **colony** of Portugal so its culture is a mixture of Indian and Portuguese traditions. The sea, beach and coastal sand-dunes support the livelihoods of local people through fishing, farming and tapping toddy. **Toddy** is a drink made from palm tree juice. In the last 30 years Goa has developed as a major tourist destination.

**B Number of visiting tourists**

| Year | No. of Tourists |
|------|-----------------|
| 1972 | 10 000 |
| 1990 | 1 000 000 |
| 2000 | 5 000 000 (estimate) |

## Why do people visit Goa?

Tourists are attracted to Goa by its natural resources, local culture and traditions, and **amenities** built for tourism. These include:
- its 105km of sandy beaches, palm-fringed beaches
- hot, dry weather in the tourist season with ten hours of daily sunshine
- direct flights from the UK to Dabolim airport
- tourist hotels backing onto the beaches.

Tourism has brought many advantages to Goa:
- construction jobs in building hotels
- jobs in hotels and other services
- improved communications systems
- income from tourism, e.g. from selling handicrafts.

But the coast is a fragile environment. In places like Goa, where many people visit one small area, tourism can have costs for local people and the environment.

**C Major tourist sites in Goa**

Key
- △ Major hotel complexes
- ▫ Main tourist beaches
- ● Towns and villages
- ‖ Bridges providing road access

'In ten years Goa will be just one long strip of hotels indistinguishable from Thailand, Miami Beach or Benidorm ... we should find somewhere else to go, with a culture that is not fragile and with very little of value that can be damaged.'

Clive Anderson, BBC film *Our Man in Goa*

**D  The down side of tourism**

**E  Climate data for Goa**

## What problems does tourism create?

Many of the changes brought by tourism affect local people's way of life. For example, sand dunes have been cleared to provide space for hotel lawns, raising fears of increased beach erosion. Some hotels have closed off access to the beach, preventing people getting access for fishing. Hotels also have a big impact on local amenities:

- a tourist in a 5-star hotel uses 28 times more electricity than a local person
- one hotel can use as much water as five villages
- some hotels get water from illegal wells, cutting local farmers water supply.

### FACTFILE

**Tourism Concern**

The increase in tourism around the world has brought new prosperity to many areas. It has also often damaged the environment and the area's traditional way of life. Hotels and tourist accommodation have been built without consideration for their surroundings. Tourists use much greater quantities of electricity and water than the local people in their own houses, sometimes causing shortages. The effect of great numbers of people on delicate environments such as coral reefs has been devastating.

Tourism Concern is a charity aiming to promote greater understanding of the impact of tourism on host communities and environments.  Its work in Goa has highlighted some of the negative impacts of tourism on this region of India. A Tourism Concern report argued that,

'Goan people are asking why they can no longer afford the high prices of some of the traditional food like fish and cashew nuts. A local women's group are protesting about how they are portrayed in the tourism literature and why they and the local carnival are being turned into a show at the expense of their dignity and culture. They are also asking why their children prefer to skip school and become involved in selling goods, often drugs, to tourists. They ask why tourists continue to insult the morality of local residents by continuing to sunbathe in the nude.'

# 5 ▶ REGIONAL AND NATIONAL DEVELOPMENT

## *Regional inequalities in India*

### ▶ Is development evenly spread across India?

You have already seen (on pages 30–31) how there are many differences in the quality of life between India's rural and urban areas. There are also differences in the quality of life across India's regions. The physical geography of many regions, such as the mountains of Kashmir or the desert areas of Rajasthan, present difficulties for development (see pages 32–33). In other areas economic policies have led to high rates of economic growth. For example, Bangalore has encouraged business development. **Adult literacy** is one of the key measures of development and the pattern across India is shown in map **A**.

'There are some poles of economic growth, notably the western states of Maharashtra (including Bombay), and Gujarat, as well as Harayana, Punjab, Goa and Karnataka (including Bangalore). There is a concentration of poverty in northern and eastern regions of Bihar, Orissa and eastern Uttar Pradesh.'

*The Economist* magazine

### *Development in Kerala*

One region which has achieved many development successes is the state of Kerala in south-west India. It is a very fertile area of India and a mainly agricultural state. The population density is high, with 76 per cent of people living in rural areas, especially in the flat land along the coast. Inland are the steep slopes of the Western Ghats (map **B**). In Kerala many farmers own their land, unlike many other states in India.

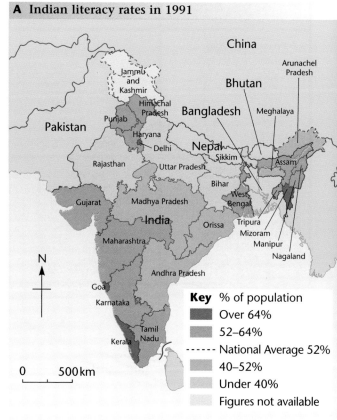

**A** Indian literacy rates in 1991

**Key** % of population
- Over 64%
- 52–64%
- ----- National Average 52%
- 40–52%
- Under 40%
- Figures not available

0    500km

The Kerala state government has an approach to development which makes people's **basic needs** and quality of life the first priority. The state government aims for the whole population to have good levels of health care and education. It has provided subsidized food and social security for the poorest, free school meals for poor school children and literacy classes for adults. For example, villages have a **ration shop** selling food and fuel at government controlled prices. K P Kannan, Professor of Development Studies, says, 'Kerala has targeted the most vulnerable among the poor such as destitute, pregnant women, children and the elderly.'

**B** Location map of Kerala

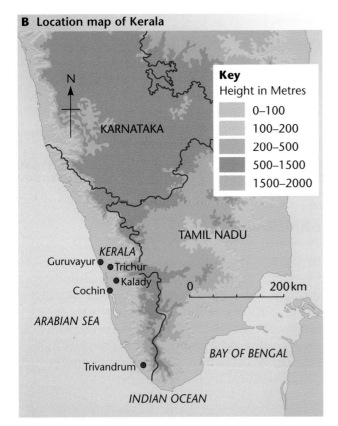

Key
Height in Metres

| | |
|---|---|
| | 0–100 |
| | 100–200 |
| | 200–500 |
| | 500–1500 |
| | 1500–2000 |

Kerala is not a wealthy state but it has achieved important successes. Infant Mortality is a third lower and its literacy levels 30 per cent higher than in the Punjab, although the Punjab is a much richer state, with incomes far higher than India's national average (table **D**). As Binu S Thomas, Researcher for ACTIONAID-India, says, 'Kerala has achieved for its 30 million people (a population the size of Canada) a quality of life comparable to the developed world, in life expectancy, literacy, population growth and infant mortality.'

| | Health beds/1000 people | Female literacy rates | Income per person as % of national average |
|---|---|---|---|
| Kerala | 44/1000 | 87% | 84% |
| Punjab (Thar Desert) | 16/1000 | 49% | 176% |
| Karnataka (Bangalore) | 9/1000 | 44% | 85% |

**C** Regional development statistics

## FACTFILE

### Kerala

Kerala is one of the most densely populated, culturally mixed and politically unusual states in the world.

- It supports a population of 29 million people, that is 747 people per square kilometre, compared with 234 in the UK.
- Its population is 60 per cent Hindu, 20 per cent Muslim and 20 per cent Christian.
- In 1957 Kerala was the first state to vote a communist government to power by democratic elections.
- Over 90 per cent of people in Kerala own the land on which their home stands.

People in Kerala live longer, thanks to better nutrition and state health care provision. Far fewer children die in their first year.

### Work and resources

- Coir (coconut fibre) accounts for 18 per cent of exports and supports 10 million people in Kerala.
- Major exports include rubber, spices, coffee, tea and cashew nuts.
- An estimated 150 000 Kerala people work in the Gulf states. They are known as 'gulfen'. Many are skilled technicians and medical staff. The money they send home makes an important contribution to the economy.
- Unemployment is the highest in India, with an estimated four million job seekers.

*The New Internationalist.*

| | Life expectancy (years) | Infant mortality (per 1000 births) |
|---|---|---|
| Kerala | 70 | 20 |
| India | 56 | 94 |
| USA | 75 | 10 |

# People involved in India's development

## ▶ Who is involved in India's development?

A wide range of people and organizations are involved in India's development. They include:
- India's people
- 50 000 Indian community development organizations, often called non-governmental organizations (NGOs)
- India's businesses
- Local, state and national government
- Aid-giving countries
- International NGOs
- International organizations like the World Bank and International Monetary Fund.

When investigating development it is important to start from local people's thinking. Local people have experience of the conditions and often already know ways of responding to the problems they face. For example, in 1974 the women of Reni in northern India stopped loggers from cutting down 12 000 sq km of forest by hugging trees. It was the start of the **Chipko** environmental movement. Professor Bina Agarwal says, 'On one occasion the Chipko women prevented the axing of an oak forest to establish a potato farm for men. This would have added five miles to the women's journey to collect fuel wood, while the money from the potatoes would have remained with the men.'

The Chipko movement helped slow down the destruction of forests and forced the Indian government to bring in environmental protection laws. The movement has won many awards and been copied in other parts of the world.

### URMUL Trust

This is an Indian NGO which was established in 1984. It is based in the desert state of Rajasthan where it runs health, education, drought relief and rural development work. It works with over 4000 families and spends almost 50 per cent of its income on supporting local community groups. These groups run a number of activities including co-operative businesses and legal aid schemes.

**B** This women's community group in the Nilgiri Hills is supported by the charity ACTIONAID. It provides the chance for women to discuss their problems and identify ways of overcoming them.

**A** By embracing trees members of the Chipko movement prevented them being felled by loggers.

## Types of aid

As well as India's own achievements there is also international support for development through aid. There are different forms of aid:

- Bilateral aid: from one country to another.
- Multilateral aid: from international organizations like the World Bank.
- Voluntary aid: from development charities like Oxfam and ACTIONAID.
- Other forms of aid: military assistance or technological support.

## British government aid to India

The British Overseas Development Administration (ODA) aims 'to improve the quality of life of people in poorer countries by contributing to sustainable development and reducing poverty and suffering'. The aid money it spends comes from money raised by taxes in the UK. In 1994 the ODA spent £2018 million on aid, about 0.3 per cent of Britain's GNP, well below the UN target of 0.7 per cent. Roughly 5 per cent of this aid was allocated to India, giving an average of £0.11 aid per Indian person.

## ACTIONAID – an international NGO

ACTIONAID has been operating in India since 1972 where it works with over one million people and spends £4 million a year. It works by providing funds, and support, to local Indian NGOs, such as the URMUL Trust, so that it can achieve 'the empowerment of the poor in the process of social development'. ACTIONAID also shares its experience with others involved in development, both within India and internationally. For example, in 1996 Amitava Mukherjee, ACTIONAID-India's Director, said that the planned United Nations Food Summit, 'should be renamed the "World Summit on Hunger" to focus attention on the urgent need to eliminate hunger and food insecurity.' Most of ACTIONAID's money is given by members of the public in countries like the UK.

## FACTFILE

### Two ways of looking at development

The Narmada River project, to bring water to a desert region of Gujarat, NW India, shows that not everybody agrees on the best path to development. The Narmada project has been planned since 1947. There are 30 large dams, 135 medium and 3000 small dams planned for irrigation, water supply and HEP.

The world's largest irrigation dam, the Sardar Sarovar Dam, is due to be complete by the year 2000. It will bring piped water to all 5614 villages and 130 towns in the region at a cost of $52.5 million. 7000 local people are employed in building the dam. The project was originally funded with loans from the World Bank.

For many people the project represents progress towards a modern India. Other Indians disagree, and many demonstrations against the dam have been held by community groups and Indian environmental organizations. They oppose the dam because it will flood farmland, villages and forests. They support smaller projects. Thousands of local people have been forcibly removed and when the dam is complete many thousands more will be displaced.

This pattern is repeated across India, where dams planned or under construction will mean that more than 700 000 people are displaced. Community and environmental groups argue that the money could be better spent on many more smaller projects based on the needs of local communities. So the conflict is between whether the best path to development is through modernization, or through grassroots development.

*The New Internationalist* and *Understanding Global Issues*

# India's changing economy

## How is India's economy changing?

**B** This car factory was funded by a joint venture between Indian and Korean producers.

### Changing employment

In the last fifty years there have been major changes in the type of jobs Indian people do (table A). While jobs in farming are still very important, urbanization and industrialization has led to the growth of secondary and tertiary employment.

**A Changes in the Economy: wealth created (% GDP)**

| Sector | 1950 | 1960 | 1970 | 1980 | 1990 | 1996 |
|---|---|---|---|---|---|---|
| Primary | 55 | 46 | 45 | 38 | 32 | 29 |
| Secondary | 15 | 21 | 22 | 26 | 28 | 29 |
| Tertiary | 30 | 33 | 33 | 36 | 40 | 42 |

### India's successes

In the 1980s and 1990s India made changes to the economy to make it easier for new industries to set up. Many new industries produced **consumer** products for sale to people in India and for export. Many were set up with the help of **transnational companies** based in Europe or the USA (photo C). These changes have led to high rates of economic growth, over 5 per cent a year, and increased foreign investment in the economy. Rent for **commercial** property in Mumbai (Bombay) is now more expensive than New York!

The growth of these industries has led to changes in the pattern of India's **imports** and **exports** (graph B). In the past India had to import many goods but its exports were small. Recently exports are growing by about 7 per cent a year, but imports are only growing by 3 per cent (photo **D**). This is because more consumer goods are produced by India's own industries, so there is less need for imports.

**C** Mumbai (Bombay) docks is the site where much of India's imports and exports take place.

50

## The downside

To help industry to grow India had to spend more money buying oil from overseas. Things were made worse when the price of oil doubled in the 1970s, and rose again in 1990. As a result India's **external debt** – the money it owes to other countries – leaped from $20 billion in 1980 to $90 billion in 1990. To pay for this debt costs India a huge amount of money every year. In 1994 the debt payments were a massive 27 per cent of the value of India's exports.

To pay for this debt India had to take out a large loan from the **International Monetary Fund** (IMF). In return for this money India agreed to change the structure of its economy. This **Structural Adjustment Plan** meant the government had to take less part in running the economy, leaving more decisions to business people. The government did this by:

*   **privatizing** or selling off state-owned business
*   reducing export tariffs and taxes
*   allowing more transnational companies to start new businesses in India
*   reducing government **subsidies** on some goods and cutting back some services
*   cutting '**red tape**', to allow easier imports and exports.

These changes helped improve the economy for businesses, but they affected the poorest people badly. India does provide a safety net to support its poorest people through health and education services and, for example, by subsidizing food and goods at certain shops.

However, the economic changes of the SAP led to cuts in jobs and wages and the government's safety net. Increased food prices have affected poor people's ability to provide for themselves.

**Village electrification**

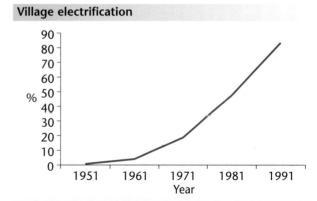

**People living below the poverty line**

| Year | Rural | Urban | Total |
| --- | --- | --- | --- |
| 1983 | 40.4 | 28.1 | 37.5 |
| 1988 | 22.5 | 14.2 | 20.4 |
| 1990 | 19.7 | 10.8 | 17.4 |
| 1992 | 22.9 | 13.0 | 20.3 |
| 1994 | 21.7 | 11.6 | 19.0 |

**Vehicle sales**

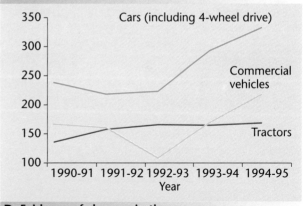

**D  Evidence of changes in the economy**

### FACTFILE

#### India's changing steel industry

India's steel industry has several advantages. It has all the major raw materials needed for a modern steel industry including:

*   12 billion tonnes of good quality iron ore, enough to last 160 years
*   8 billion tonnes of coaking coal, enough to last 100 years
*   large amounts of limestone and manganese ore
*   a skilled workforce.

India has seven large integrated steel plants and nearly 200 smaller furnaces. India's steel industry has been protected from foreign competition by high taxes on imports and it has a number of out dated and inefficient plants. The government is reducing controls and encouraging the industry to modernize and expand rapidly.

| Crude Steel Production | |
| --- | --- |
| | million tonnes |
| 1950/51 | 1.50 |
| 1960/61 | 3.42 |
| 1970/71 | 6.30 |
| 1980/81 | 9.39 |
| 1990/91 | 14.92 |
| 1999/2000 | 35.00 |

*United Nations Industrial Development Organization*

# Development trends in India

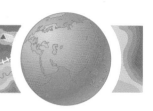

## Fifty years of progress

Despite the many problems facing India it has made great strides in development. One of the key signs of progress is that India is now self-sufficient in food and often exports food grains. Only 50 years ago millions of people were affected by famine and India had to rely on food aid from foreign countries.

Over the same period India has established itself as the world's largest democratic country. This allows people to freely express their views about changes taking place in their country and hold their leaders accountable at elections. As *The Economist* magazine reports, 'Although literacy levels are low, villagers throughout India discuss politics with great enthusiasm. But they are also doubtful about the promises given to them before each election and use their votes carefully.'

## How does this affect people?

These changes affect individuals, as well as countries. Sukhdev Patil from Asegaon village, Maharashtra, says, 'That's my well and where I grow vegetables. They are a priority because I can feed my family and sell what's left over. Before this my children hardly knew the taste of vegetables.'

The general increase in people's wealth can be seen in the growing demand for consumer goods in India. In 1994 Indians owned more than 77 million bicycles, 40 million TVs, and 64 million radios, to name just a few products. Other improvements can be seen in the box on the next page.

**A** A polling booth in Delhi during India's recent general election.

# Does economic development improve quality of life?

**B** India's development achievements

### Literacy rate

|         | 1951(%) | 1995(%) |
|---------|---------|---------|
| Total   | 20      | 52      |
| Men     | 27      | 64      |
| Women   | 9       | 36      |

(* India now has over 10 million university graduates)

### Infant Mortality Rate

| 1947     | 1960     | 1995    |
|----------|----------|---------|
| 270/1000 | 144/1000 | 70/1000 |

### Life expectancy

| 1947     | 1995     |
|----------|----------|
| 27 years | 62 years |

It should not be forgotten that almost 30 per cent of India's population still live below the government's poverty line and in 1990 40 per cent of the world's poorest people lived in India.

| 1977 | 78 305 million |
|------|----------------|
| 1987 | 88 240 million |
| 1993 | 94 169 million |

**C** People living in poverty

Whatever the approach the important question should always be: 'How is the quality of people's lives affected?' For example, as the economy grows more wealth is created, but the question is how is it shared by different groups in society? (table **D**)

'There is evidence that economic growth does not always improve the quality of life. The environmental destruction and loss of livelihoods caused by mining and major irrigation projects have done more harm than good to the quality of life of the poor, regardless of rises in GNP.'

Binu S Thomas, ACTIONAID-India

## FACTFILE

### Democracy

Since independence in 1947 democracy has become firmly embedded in Indian society. Every time India holds a general election it enters the Guinness Book of Records for sending the most voters to the polls. In 1991, more than 514 million Indians cast their votes, about four times the number of voters in India's first election after independence in 1952.

Indian elections are on such a scale that it takes several days to count all the votes. To ensure that all those eligible can vote, whether they can read or not, each party has a symbol which voters recognize and can mark their vote against. For example the Congress Party uses a hand held in greeting and the Lok Dal, a party which draws votes from agricultural workers,

uses the image of two cows and a farmer ploughing. India's first democratically elected Prime Minister was Jawaharlal Nehru, who led India from 1947 to 1964. His party, the Congress Party, has held power for most of the period since independence.

The Congress Party is one of the world's oldest political parties. But there are numerous other political parties in India, representing different regional, religious, class and political groupings. In contrast the colours of the Indian flag represent unity: saffron yellow is the colour of Hinduism and Buddhism, green is the colour of Islam, and the wheel of life is at the centre.

# 6 INDIA'S FUTURE

## India and the global community

### ▶ Can India follow the Asian Tigers?

Despite India's huge size it only accounts for just under 1 per cent of world trade (map **B**). India's recent economic changes have increased the amount of its manufactured exports, such as electronic goods (table **E**). Other Asian countries have also been developing their manufacturing industries, particularly Hong Kong (now part of China), Taiwan, Singapore and South Korea. These four countries, known as the Asian Tigers, have built up very successful economies based on the export of manufactured products. They have very quickly moved from relatively poor nations to what are known as **Newly Industrialized Countries** (NICS).

### Access to overseas markets
Many people have wondered whether India could match their success. As Manmohan Singh, India's Minister of Finance in 1991, said 'Why does everyone talk about South Korea? This is because in 1960, South Korea had the same income per person as India. Today, South Korea's income is ten times India's!'

**A** Air-freight provides rapid access for Indian goods to the global market.

One of the problems for the NICs, and also for India, is whether they can get access to overseas markets where they can sell their products. More countries are joining up to form trading blocks such as the EU and the North American Trade Association, NAFTA (map **B**). It is often difficult for countries like India to gain access to these markets. For example, India's export of textiles to America increased by 65 per cent during the early 1990s, but in future NAFTA may restrict India's exports. A representative from the American

**B** World trading blocks

Key
- EU (European Union)
- NAFTA (North American Free Trade Organization)
- ASEAN (Association of South East Asian Nations)
- CACM (Central American Common Market)
- OPEC (Organisation of Petroleum Exporting Countries)

Textile Manufacturers says, 'We see NAFTA as very positive because it can reduce the Asian Imports.'

The demand for some exports like basic electrical goods produced by the NICs is also limited. The NICs have been able to overcome this by changing to produce new goods such as high-tech equipment. This process is starting in Bangalore (see pages 42–43).

Some people do not believe the low wages paid to workers in many manufacturing industries will be good enough for long-term economic growth. Mr Dang from Hindustani Computers says, 'Low salaries are not going to sustain growth. What is going to count is professional competence, using our skills and technology.'

## C  Changes in the proportion of world trade (%)

| | 1970 | 1990 |
|---|---|---|
| EU | 48 | 43 |
| USA | 13 | 15 |
| Japan | 10 | 13 |
| Developing countries | 4.5 | 10 |
| India | 0.5 | 1 |
| Newly industrialized countries | 4 | 9 |
| Others | 20 | 12 |

## D  Destination of India's exports 1994–95 (%)

| | |
|---|---|
| USA | 19 |
| Japan | 8 |
| Germany | 7 |
| UK | 6 |
| Russia | 3 |
| France | 2 |
| Other developed countries | 16 |
| OPEC | 9 |
| Eastern Europe | 4 |
| Developing Countries | 24 |
| Others | 4 |

## E  Composition of India's imports and exports 1991 (%)

| | Imports | Exports |
|---|---|---|
| **Total** *(Million $US)* | 19,509 | 17,900 |
| Food/live animals | 2.0 | 15.2 |
| Drinks/tobacco | 0.0 | 0.9 |
| Crude materials/non–food | 7.7 | 7.2 |
| Mineral fuels, lubricants etc. | 30 | 2.4 |
| Animal/vegetable oils/ fats | 0.7 | 0.4 |
| Chemicals | 15.8 | 8.4 |
| Manufactured goods | 19.4 | 37.5 |
| Machinery/transport equipment | 13.5 | 7.5 |
| Misc. manufactured goods | 2.9 | 19.0 |
| Misc. transactions and goods | 8.0 | 1.6 |

## CHARACTERISTICS OF NICS

- Manufacturing production is growing fast – mainly for export
- Few government controls in the economy
- Low wages
- Education and training very important
- Small farming sector with less than 10 per cent income from agriculture
- Population and population growth less than 1.5 per cent.

## FACTFILE

### A changing world order

### 'Developing World to Eclipse Europe says World Bank'

The Big Five developing countries – Brazil, China, India, Indonesia and Russia - will transform the world economic map over the next 25 years as they first catch up and then overtake Europe in terms of global trade, a report from the World Bank claims.

The Bank is upbeat about the prospects for developing countries - including those who have experienced declining rather than rising standards in recent years. It forecasts that the economies of developing countries as a whole will grow twice as fast between now and 2006. In 1913 developing countries accounted for 16.5 per cent of the world' total Gross Domestic Product. By 1995 this had grown to 18 per cent and is projected to reach 33 per cent by the year 2020.

*The Daily Telegraph*, 10 September 1997

# The prospects for India's development

▶ **What are the difficulties facing India's development?**

You have seen many of the challenges facing India's development prospects, including:
- its monsoon climate (pages 10–11)
- the size and diversity of its population (pages 16–19)
- the size of India's debt (pages 50–51)
- high rates of poverty (pages 36–37)
- high rates of rural–urban migration (pages 20–21).

Other challenges facing India include:

## Historical
After almost 200 years of extracting India's wealth, by exporting its raw materials or selling British goods to its people, power was handed over from the British to India in 1947. They left behind a farming system which could not feed its own people, few industries and a population with low levels of education and health.

At the end of British rule, India was divided into two countries. India became a largely Hindu nation and a new Muslim state, Pakistan, was founded. This created massive disruption as 15 million people moved from one country to another. It also created friction between India and Pakistan, leading to a number of armed conflicts. Distrust continues between the two countries today.

## Social problems
From time to time there is tension between India's different religions. For example in 1992, a dispute between Hindus and Muslims over the situation of a mosque and temple at Ayodhya, turned into rioting throughout India. India has also suffered tension in some of its own states such as Kashmir.

## Water supply
More irrigation has provided better water supplies for many farmers, but in places too much water has been **extracted** so the level of **underground water** has been lowered. The United Nations has reported that India's ground water is being extracted faster than it is **recharged**.

To increase water supplies in the area around Calcutta, India has built a barrage across the River Ganges at Farakka. But the River Ganges also flows through Bangladesh, which means there is less water for irrigation and drinking for people there.

## Deforestation
Only 6.5 per cent of rural households have mains electricity, so people need another source of fuel for heating and cooking. The most common fuel in rural areas is wood and this has placed great demands on forests. India's forests are also under threat from logging and other forms of exploitation.

**A** A train taking Muslims to the new Muslim country of Pakistan, which was created by the partition of India in 1947.

**B** Deforestation has lead to high rates of soil erosion in parts of the Himalayas.

## THE SHRINKING FORESTS OF INDIA

Concern is growing about India's forests', which shrank at a rate of 0.6 percent during the 1980s. Agricultural land has suffered as the fertile soil is washed away. Deforestation is blamed for flash floods , inadequate recharging of underground water supplies and silted-up rivers

**C** Newspaper article on deforestation

## *Natural disasters*

'Natural disasters in India have included rampaging floods, when rivers extended their watery grip over large areas of land, and scorching droughts, which have left behind festering sores on once fertile lands.'

The Indian Centre for Science and Environment

## FACTFILE

### Transport

India is a very large country and needs a network of roads and railways to transport goods and people hundreds of miles every day. The road system is still in need of considerable improvement. Over 60 000 people are killed on India's roads each year:

'Although the rail and postal systems are quite impressive and ports, air services and tele-communications are improving, roads are generally quite unsuited to modern requirements. While India has about one million km of surfaced roads, over one-third of villages have no road link and 70 per cent have no 'all-weather' links. The quality of roads, even the national motorways, is generally appalling by international standards. They are narrow, badly maintained, highly congested, slow and dangerous. The number of vehicles has risen from 300,000 in 1950/51 to 31 million in 1995/96.'

*The Economist, 1997.*

Only a small proportion of the population own cars. The vast majority travel by bus or train. More than ten million travel on India's 62 210km of rail network every day. There are still some steam locomotives in use, and the longest journey of 3733km from Jammu in the north to Kanya Kumari in the south takes 89 hours.

# India's future

**A** A family in Rajasthan preparing for their son's marriage.

Fifty years ago India was ruled by a colonial power, had few industries of its own and was barely able to feed itself. Today, India has made huge improvements in the quality of life for its people.

'In its industrial and technological achievements it is arguably a giant. Its industrial expertise extends into such advanced fields as nuclear energy, satellites and software design.'

*The Economist* magazine

Many influences will shape India's future. These include:

## DE-COLONIZATION

Many of the colonial names for places are being changed. This has happened in Bombay, where *bombaim* – Portuguese for a good harbour – became the English word Bombay. The new Indian name is Mumbai. Sushila Singh says, 'The changes are a way for people to show their Indianess by getting rid of the colonial legacy.'

## DEMOCRACY

India has remained as a democratic country for over 50 years. This is important because it allows its people to express ideas openly, debate them, vote for their own government and hold their politicians accountable to the people.

## TOURISM

Two million tourists a year visit India bringing $1.5 billion into the economy. Tourists range from backpackers, getting by on a few dollars a day, to those booking 5-star hotels. However, *The Economist* magazine reported that 'India has barely tapped its vast tourism potential with under 0.4 per cent of the world's tourists and around 1 per cent of tourist spending.' To encourage tourism, new hotels have been built, more international flights scheduled, and better communications have been developed.

## So what will the future bring?

From the pastoral farmers of the Thar deserts to Bangalore's bustling computer factories across India people are working to improve their quality of life and for better conditions.

However, as you have seen, there are many human and physical geographical processes which influence how these changes affect India's people.

**B** India has successfully launched its own satellites and high-tech industries are well established.

### FACTFILE

**India and the world**

|  | Real GNP growth per capita (1985-91) | 1994 GNP per capita (in US$) |
|---|---|---|
| Thailand | 8.2 | 6870 |
| S. Korea | 7.8 | 10540 |
| China | 6.9 | 2510 |
| Indonesia | 6.0 | 3690 |
| Japan | 3.2 | 21350 |
| India | 2.9 | 1290 |
| Bangladesh | 2.1 | 1350 |
| Pakistan | 1.6 | 2210 |

'In the last decade or so the Eastern Tiger economies leapfrogged over the stage of industrial development and pushed into the information age. Singapore, for example, has the world's most sophisticated telecommunications infrastructure and is a centre for multinational computer firms. Hong Kong's rule in global finance equals that of London or New York. Singapore is a world leader in manufacturing sophisticated, high-tech quality products. As we move towards the 21st century, Asia will become the dominant region of the world technologically, economically, politically, culturally and militarily. Until the 1990s the West set their own rules for the Asians; this is no longer so. Asians are creating their own rules.'
*Dr Amitava Mukherjee, Director, ACTIONAID-India.*

# Statistics

| | UK | ITALY | BRAZIL | JAPAN | INDIA |
|---|---|---|---|---|---|
| Total area (km²) | 244 100 | 301 270 | 8 511 965 | 377 801 | 3 287 260 |
| Total population (millions) | 58.3 | 57.2 | 159.1 | 125.2 | 943.0 |
| Population density: people per km² | 241 | 194 | 19 | 332 | 317 |

## Population

| | UK | ITALY | BRAZIL | JAPAN | INDIA |
|---|---|---|---|---|---|
| Birth rate per 1000 people | 14 | 11 | 26 | 10 | 31 |
| Death rate per 1000 people | 12 | 11 | 8 | 6 | 10 |
| Life expectancy (male and female) | 73M 79F | 73M 80F | 64M 69F | 76M 83F | 60M 61F |
| Fertility (children per female) | 2 | 1 | 3 | 2 | 4 |
| Population structure 0–14 / 15–59 / 60+ | 19% 60% 21% | 17% 63% 20% | 35% 58% 7% | 19% 64% 17% | 37% 56% 7% |
| Urban population | 89% | 67% | 76% | 77% | 26% |

## Environment and economy

| | UK | ITALY | BRAZIL | JAPAN | INDIA |
|---|---|---|---|---|---|
| Rate of urban growth per year | 0.3% | 0.6% | 2.3% | 0.6% | 2.9% |
| Land use: arable / grass / forest | 27% 46% 10% | 31% 17% 23% | 7% 22% 58% | 11% 2% 67% | 56% 4% 23% |
| % of workforce in: farming / industry / services | 2 28 70 | 9 32 59 | 25 25 50 | 7 34 59 | 62 11 27 |
| GNP per person (US$) | $17 970 | $19 620 | $2 920 | $31 450 | $290 |
| Unemployment | 9.4% | 11.6% | 5.9% | 3.0% | n/a |
| Energy used (tonnes/person/year) | 5.40 | 4.02 | 0.44 | 4.74 | 0.35 |

## Society and quality of life

| | UK | ITALY | BRAZIL | JAPAN | INDIA |
|---|---|---|---|---|---|
| Infant mortality (deaths per 1000 births) | 8 | 9 | 57 | 5 | 88 |
| People per doctor | 300 | 211 | 1000 | 600 | 2439 |
| Food supply (calories per person per day) | 3317 | 3561 | 2824 | 2903 | 2395 |
| Adult literacy | 99% | 97% | 81% | 99% | 50% |
| TVs per 1000 people | 434 | 421 | 207 | 613 | 35 |
| Aid received or given per person | $50 given | $53 given | $1.2 received | $90 given | $1.7 received |
| Education spending (% of GNP) | 5.3 | 4.1 | n/a | 5.0 | 3.5 |
| Military spending (% of GNP) | 4.0 | 2.0 | n/a | 1.0 | 2.5 |
| United Nations Human Development Index (out of 1.0) | 0.92 | 0.91 | 0.80 | 0.94 | 0.44 |

Figures are for 1992–95. Source: *Philip's Geographical Digest* (United Nations, World Bank). The Human Development Index is worked out by the UN. It is a summary of national income, life expectancy, adult literacy and education. It is a measure of human progress. In 1992, HDI ranged from 0.21 to 0.94.

## General

Longest river: Ganges (2510km)
Highest mountain: Kangchenjunga (8598m)
Largest city: Bombay (now Mumbai)
(12.6 million)
Capital: New Delhi
Languages: 18 official languages, 1 634 'mother tongues'; Hindi (30%), English, Telugu (8%), Bengali (8%), Marati (8%), Urdu (5%)
Currency: Rupees
Religion: Hindu (80%), Muslim (11%), Christian (2%), Sikh (2%), Buddhist (1%)

### Population of largest cities

| Bombay (now Mumbai) | 12 600 000 |
|---|---|
| Calcutta | 10 900 000 |
| Delhi | 7 200 000 |
| Madras | 5 400 000 |
| Bangalore | 4 000 000 |
| Ahmadabad | 3 300 000 |
| Pune | 2 500 000 |
| Kanpur | 2 100 000 |
| Nagpur | 1 700 000 |
| Lucknow | 1 600 000 |
| Jaipur | 1 500 000 |

### Some of India's major industries

| | 000 tonnes | World ranking |
|---|---|---|
| Iron | 55 600 | 5 |
| Steel | 18 500 | 11 |
| Aluminium | 466 | 14 |
| Fertilizers | 9 787 | 3 |

### India's major crops (1993)

| | 000 tonnes | World ranking |
|---|---|---|
| Tea | 758 | 1 |
| Cotton | 4270 | 3 |
| Jute | 1500 | 1 |
| Tobacco | 581 | 4 |
| Coffee | 169 | 9 |
| Sugar | 11 535 | 1 |
| Wheat | 56 762 | 3 |
| Rice | 111 011 | 2 |
| Millet | 10 000 | 1 |

### Total consumption of fertilizers (1992)

| | 000 tonnes | World ranking |
|---|---|---|
| India | 12 218 | 3 |
| USA | 18 983 | 2 |
| China | 29 155 | 1 |

## Economic

### Imports and exports (%) (1991)

| | Imports | Exports |
|---|---|---|
| Food and live animals | 2.0 | 15.2 |
| Beverages and tobacco | 0.0 | 0.9 |
| Crude materials (excluding fuels) | 7.7 | 7.2 |
| Mineral fuels, lubricants | 30.0 | 2.4 |
| Animals and vegetables oils and fats | 0.7 | 0.4 |
| Chemicals | 15.8 | 8.4 |
| Manufactured goods (textiles, etc.) | 19.4 | 37.5 |
| Machinery and transport equipment | 13.5 | 7.5 |
| Miscellaneous goods | 10.9 | 20.6 |
| Total (million US $) | 22 763 | 21 554 |

### Access to safe water and sanitation (%)

| | Safe Water | Sanitation |
|---|---|---|
| India | 81 | 29 |
| UK | 99 | 99 |
| USA | 99 | 99 |

### Transport

| | Roads (per 1000 sq km) | Railways (per 1000 sq km) |
|---|---|---|
| India | 325 | 21 |
| UK | 1500 | 70 |
| USA | 380 | 25 |
| Australia | 32 | 5 |

# Glossary

**adult literacy** the number of people who can read and write per 1000 of the population

**alluvial** a type of fine mud or silt deposited by rivers

**altitude(s)** height above sea level

**amenities** purpose-built facilities

**appropriate technology** the use of small-scale simple tools which are more useful to people in rural areas

**basic needs** things like food, shelter and health care

**birth rate** number of live births per 1000 of population

**castes** a system of social groups which people are born into, traditionally they were associated with particular jobs

**central business district (CBD)** the central part of a town or city containing offices and shops

**Chipko** An environmental movement which started when Indian women began to 'hug' trees to prevent them being felled

**collision plate margin** this is where two plates collide or push together causing massive earthquakes

**colony** a country which is under the control of a more powerful one

**commercial** for use by businesses

**common land** land which is used by everyone in a community, such as for grazing

**consumer** person who buys and uses a product

**consumer goods** items for sale directly to the public

**crust** the earth's is its outer layer. Below the earth's crust the rocks are in a semi-molten state

**death rate** number of deaths per 1000 of population

**diversity** the variation within a country, such as cultural, ethnic, religious or linguistic

**earthquake** unpredictable movements in the earth which cause the ground to shake and which can be strong enough to destroy buildings

**economically active** these are people within a country's population who are of working age

**eroded** top soil can be removed through the action of water or wind

**exports** the sale of goods produced in one country to another

**external debt** the amount owed to other countries

**extracted** removed or taken out of

**farm labour** the actual work on the farm

**fertilizers** any material used to fertilize soil

**fold mountains** when two plates collide the land between them is forced upwards to form 'fold' mountains

**food crops** crops, such as wheat or rice, which are grown for people to eat

**Green Revolution** A series of changes which took place in Indian agriculture using a high technology approach, such as the sue of chemical fertilizers and high yeilding varieties of crops, to increase crop production

**Gross National Product (GNP)** this is a measure of the amount of wealth produced by a country each year. GNP/capita shows the average amount of wealth each person within a country has

**ground water** Water found below the surface in a permeable rock

**high-tech** high technology

**high yielding varieties (HYVs)** new types of crops which have been scientifically developed to produce a greater harvest. HYVs often need chemical fertlizers to produce a good crop

**imports** goods and services coming into a country

**indigo** a type of plant from which a deep-blue dye is extracted

**informal settlements** areas where people, often new migrants in an urban area, have built homes on land without permission

**integrated iron and steel plants** both types of manufacturing in one location

**International Monetary Fund (IMF)** an organization set up to help countries' economies

**large-scale industries** where many people are employed in many locations

**location** where an industry or firm is set up

**Latur** this is a place name

**migrants** people who have moved from one place to another, such as from a rural to an urban area

**migrations** the movement of people (or animals) from one place to another

**monsoon** the season which brings the main rains to India

**mountain chain** range of mountains linked together

**nationalized** industries which are owned and run by a country's government

**natural increase** the increase in population caused by the difference between the birth and death rate

**Newly Industrialised Countries (NICs)** this is the name given to a group of countries in Asia which have moved relatively quickly from being less developed nations to having successful economies based on the export of manufactured products

**peri-urban growth** the growth of settlements on the edges of urban areas. These settlements often have both rural and urban characteristics

**pesticides** chemical substances used to kill insects or animals that are seen as harmful to people or crops

**plantations** Large estates on which crops, such as tea or coffee, are grown for sale

**plates** The earth's crust is divided into large areas called plates. These plates float on the semi-molten rocks below them

**privatizing** transferring state-owned businesses to the private sector

**ration shop** a shop with goods to be distributed at controlled prices

**raw materials** a primary or partly processed product which is the basis of the finished item

**recharged** replaced or re-supplied

**'red tape'** paperwork and administration

**Richter Scale** this is used to measure the strength of an earthquake

**small-scale** using few people and resources to produce something

**sorghum** this is a grain food crop

**Structural Adjustment Plan** condition of a loan from IMF

**subsidies** where government keeps prices artificially low

**tariffs** duties or taxes to be paid on imports and exports

**'tax breaks'** a form of encouragement to businesses

**Toddy** a drink made from palm tree juice

**trade barriers** these are laws which control what can be brought in and out of a country 38/39

**transnational companies (TNCs)** companies with their Head Offices in other countries

**underground water** water below the water table

**urban bias** where the cities have more favourable rates of pay etc

**water table** the level underground below which the ground is saturated with water

# Index

Bold type refers to terms
included in the glossary